Southern Living

THE OFFICIAL **SEC**

Tailgating
COOKBOOK

Oxmoor House

Southern Living

THE OFFICIAL **SEC**

Tailgating
COOKBOOK

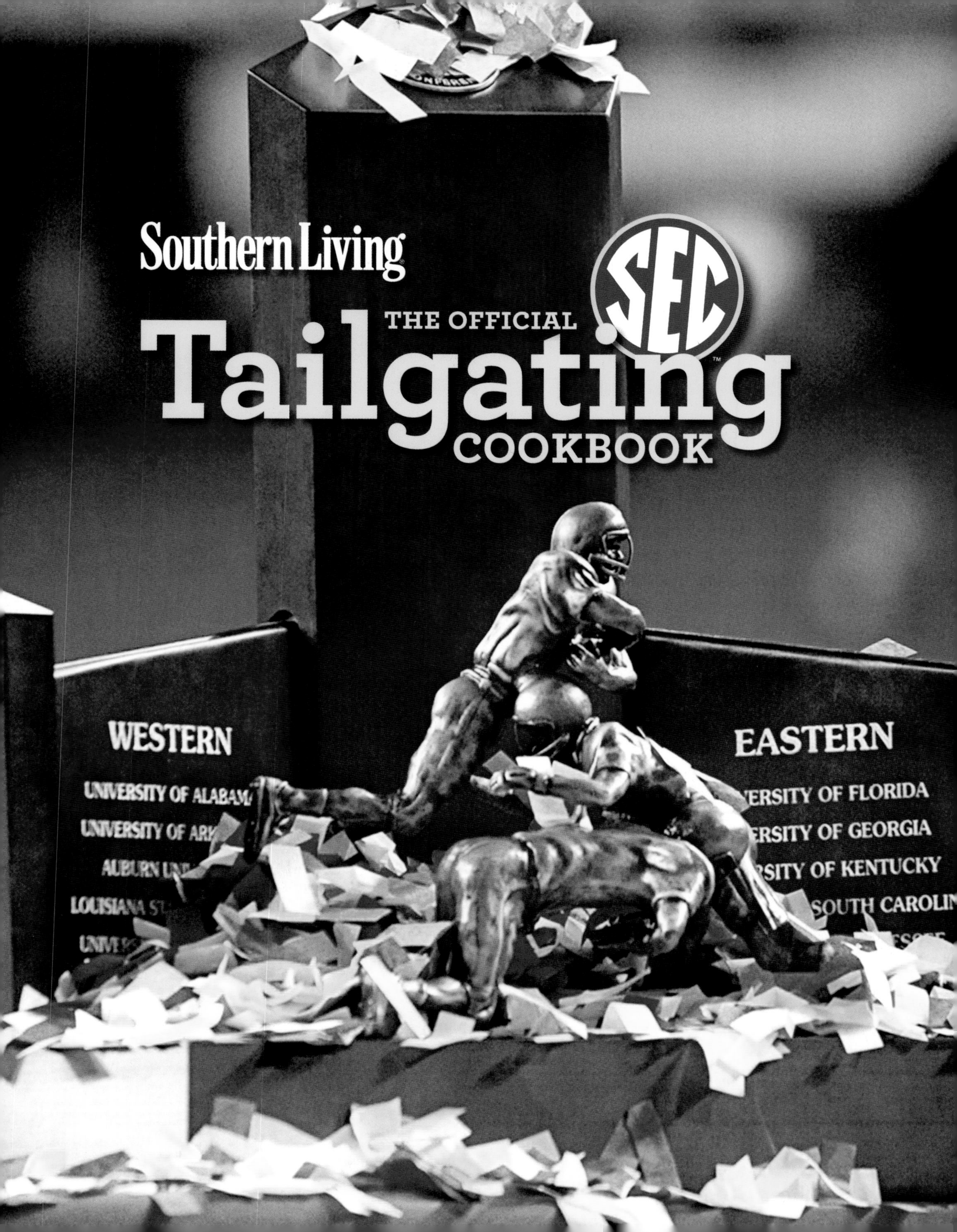

WESTERN

UNIVERSITY OF ALABAMA

UNIVERSITY OF ARK

AUBURN UNI

LOUISIANA ST

UNIV

EASTERN

...VERSITY OF FLORIDA

...ERSITY OF GEORGIA

...RSITY OF KENTUCKY

...SOUTH CAROLIN

...ESSE

CONTENTS

Foreword

> "The passion that people in the South have for the sport goes beyond what most would consider normal. We don't just play games; we host all-day events."
> —University of Georgia head coach MARK RICHT

In my 15 years of covering college football for *Sports Illustrated*, I've witnessed scores of tailgating scenes. But there is nothing—NOTHING—that compares to tailgating in the SEC, where at every school the parties are virtually as important as the games. Why? Because in SEC country, the 60 minutes of action on the field is only a fraction of the overall experience of a football Saturday.

In Tuscaloosa, the must-see tailgating stop is the Quad, where hundreds of tents are set up and fans will eat pig roasts before playing the Razorbacks and fried gator before taking on Florida. In Auburn, an armada of RVs adorned with Tiger flags will descend on campus on Tuesdays before home games—more than 100 hours before kickoff. And in Knoxville, Tennessee, a flotilla of more than 100 boats will dock on the Tennessee River just outside of Neyland Stadium where, win or lose, the tailgating will go deep into the night.

There is even romance at the SEC tailgate. In 2006, my close friend, Brian Shinnick, had his first date with Kathy Harris at The Grove at Ole Miss. The 10-acre meadow in Oxford, which is shaded by oaks, elms, and magnolia trees, is to tailgating what Cézanne is to still lifes: pristine and near perfect. With the women outfitted in brightly colored sundresses, the men in ties and slacks, and tents sprouting as far as the eye can see, The Grove on football Saturdays is tailgating as an art form.

And so two years after Brian (an Auburn grad) and Kathy (an Ole Miss alum) met for the first time at The Grove, they returned for another Rebels-Tigers game. Under a tent, an hour after Ole Miss won 17-7, Brian dropped to a knee in front of his family and friends and asked Kathy for her hand in marriage. Tears filling her eyes, she said "yes."

"Every good Ole Miss girl wants to get engaged in The Grove at a tailgate," says Brian with a laugh. Once the ring was on Kathy's finger, everyone in the tent went back to sipping their drink of choice and munching on seven-layer dip. The party, after all, was just getting started.

—Lars Anderson is a writer for *Sports Illustrated* and author of five books.

Welcome

I'll admit it. I'm an obsessed fan during football season. My die-hard devotion to team and tailgating is intense. But what unites me with all SEC fans is the love for the game and the promise and expectation of good eats.

Whether you're a season ticket holder or whether you plan to host a house full of fans in front of the television, with *Southern Living The Official SEC Tailgating Cookbook* in hand, your tailgate party—regardless of location—is sure to be a winning success.

Early morning kickoff? No problem. Make-ahead options? We've got you covered. You'll find menus for each of the 14 Southeastern Conference football teams as well as valuable insider info on how to throw the best tailgate in the South. It's a playbook, if you will, of everything you need to know in order to pull off an event with grace and ease.

Trust me, I know it can be tough getting out of town on game day. I'm the one behind you in traffic on the interstate—my SUV is decked out with car flags, pom-poms peeking from the tailgate, complete with university tag. I'm fully aware that a game plan is a must. Not only will you find the most comprehensive tailgating ideas, we've also included secret strategies and trick plays called "Extra Points" to help pull off your game-day spread.

Everyone wants to be invited to be a part of something grand, spectacular, and richly rooted in tradition. My policy has always been all-inclusive when it comes to tailgating over plates of barbecue and platters of fried chicken, whether it's shared with friends or even strangers. So get ready for a season-long party each football Saturday in the fall, and join me in celebrating one of the South's oldest traditions.

Ruecca Kracke Gordon

—Rebecca Kracke Gordon is an SEC football fanatic, tailgate strategist, and *Southern Living* Test Kitchen Director.

> Tailgating. It's become the ultimate family reunion or party across the South, and the great thing about it is that everyone's invited.

(1)
COUNTDOWN TO KICKOFF

Pitch your tent, lower your tailgate, and celebrate the best time of the year in the South. Discover all you need to know for perfect grilling, food safety, and transporting your winning selections.

Get Fired Up!

The aroma of food cooking over an open fire gives new meaning to the game-day chant "Get fired up!" For truly winning recipes—tailgate style—set up your grill and get to it!

Get the Fire Going

For gas grills, simply ignite the burners and preheat the grill to the correct temperature specified in the recipe. If you're using indirect heat, turn off one side of the grill once it's preheated. For charcoal grills, follow these steps:

1. Light the charcoal. A chimney starter is indispensable for charcoal grilling. Stuff newspaper in the bottom, place charcoal in the top, and light the paper. Now wait until the coals catch fire. Avoid using lighter fluid because it can give food a bitter flavor. If you don't see smoke pouring out of the top and, eventually, flames, you need to relight.

2. Wait, and then wait a bit more. Yes, it can take its sweet time. But don't rush: Allow the flames to die down and the coals to take on a bright red glow with a gray, ashy look. These cues signal that it's time to put down your beverage and dump the coals into the bottom of the grill.

3. Spread the bed of coals. Arrange the coals in a pattern for indirect or direct heat suited to what you're cooking. For veggies that take longer than 20 minutes to cook (such as dense potatoes), pile coals to one side of the grill for indirect heat. For quicker-cooking ingredients, pile coals in the center of the grill for direct heat.

Keep It Clean

Each time you grill, preheat the rack with all burners on high for 10 to 15 minutes to incinerate any remaining residue from the last cookout, making it easy to clean off. Then brush the grate with a grill brush. Clean the grates vigorously so they're smooth and free of food that may have stuck from your previous grilling session.

Essential Grilling Tools

Keep a box of grilling essentials handy so all you have to do is grab them and go. A clear plastic container with a lid works great. Fill it with an array of grilling tools such as two pairs of long-handled tongs (one pair for placing raw items on the grill and one pair for removing cooked items), oven mitt or grill gloves, thermometer, grill brush, long matches, and a spatula.

Feeling the Heat?

When determining if your grill is preheated to the right temperature, place your hand, palm side down, 5 inches above the grate, and count how long you can comfortably hold it there.

7 to 8 seconds = medium-low (250° to 300°)

5 to 6 seconds = medium (300° to 350°)

3 to 4 seconds = medium-high (350° to 400°)

2 seconds or less = high (400° to 450°)

The Complete Tailgating Food Safety Playbook

Serious football fans believe in seriously fun tailgating, so don't leave anything to chance when you head for the stadium. Because tailgate parties are usually all-day food fests and grilling extravaganzas, they're also a time of increased risk of food poisoning. Before you pack your cooler and head off to the game, remember these simple food safety tips.

- Keep hot food hot and keep cold food cold. Pack food in a well-insulated cooler with plenty of ice or ice packs to keep the temperature below 40°. Transport the cooler in the back seat of your air-conditioned car instead of in your hot trunk and keep your cooler closed tight. For hot food, keep and transport in a casserole carrier, slow cooker, or thermos.

- Take food in the smallest quantity needed. Pack only the amount of food you think you'll eat. Consider taking along non-perishable foods and snacks that don't need to be refrigerated.

- Pack several smaller coolers to keep raw food separate from already prepared foods. Designate another that can be opened more often for drinks.

- Bring moist towelettes or soap and water to clean your hands and surfaces often.

- Remove from the cooler only the amount of raw meat, fish, or poultry that will fit on the grill at one time.

- Cook foods to the correct temperature by using a meat thermometer: hamburgers to at least 160° and chicken breasts to 165°.

- Don't let food sit out for more than one hour. On a hot day (90° or higher), reduce this time to 30 minutes. Nestle platters and bowls filled with mayonnaise-based deviled eggs and potato salad into larger bowls filled with ice. Keep bugs at bay by placing plastic wrap or foil directly over food until ready to serve.

- When the tailgate is over, discard all perishable foods if there is no longer sufficient ice in the cooler or if ice packs are no longer frozen.

Fan-Favorite Game-Day Dishes

The food that Southern tailgaters eat on football Saturday is almost as important as who wins the big game. Traditional recipes, such as sweet tea and chocolate chip cookies, always have season tickets, while others are simply local favorites. Whichever dishes you choose, they're all surefire winners.

SOUTHERN SWEET TEA (page 50) Here's a universally Southern favorite. No matter where you tailgate in the South, you'll find this thirst quencher gracing just about every table.

SPICY BUFFALO WINGS (page 157) Hot wings may be the quintessential game-day food. Round it out with Spicy Buffalo Sauce and Cool Ranch Sauce. And don't forget the celery.

FRIED CHICKEN BITES (page 85) These perfect picnic bites will win over the hungriest football fanatics.

LAYERED SPICY BLACK BEAN DIP (page 91) Grab some chips and hit the road. Here's a portable dip that transports well.

SUPER-QUICK CHILI (page 120) Prepare this on game day and keep it warm in a slow cooker. Invest in a set of white mugs to serve the chili in, and dress up the handles with your team colors.

MAMA'S FRIED CHICKEN (page 158) You can't beat Southern fried chicken for a day of football fun. Feel free to fry a day ahead and enjoy it picnic-style.

SLOW-COOKER BARBECUE PORK (page 153) Topped with Creamy Slaw, a pork sandwich on game day is a no-brainer.

SWEET-HOT BABY BACK RIBS (page 152) Nothing can compete with this first-string rib recipe. Your friends and family will be coming back for more.

PIMIENTO CHEESE-BACON BURGERS (page 139) Pimiento cheese. Bacon. Burgers. Three Southern classics. There's not much more to say. Delish!

ROOT BEER BAKED BEANS (page 185) You are guaranteed to find baked beans at just about every tailgating affair. We like ours with root beer, making them sweet and deliciously good.

BLT POTATO SALAD (page 186) Potato salad is a tailgate standard, but there's no standard recipe. Other favorites include creamy with a base of mustard and mayo, a version with sliced, skin-on new potatoes, and mayo-based flavored with sweet pickles.

MISSISSIPPI HUSH PUPPIES (page 174) Standard tailgate fare in Mississippi and South Carolina includes these crisp cornmeal nuggets. But you don't have to be from those two states to appreciate the fried-up goodness.

CRANBERRY-ALMOND COLESLAW (page 185) Cabbage slaw is a definite at tailgates—and, for some, a must on top of the meat in a sandwich. Still, the coleslaw variations are endless. We like this dressed-up version.

ALL-TIME FAVORITE CHOCOLATE CHIP COOKIES (page 221) It wouldn't be a tailgate without some cookies to nibble on. And what could be better than chocolate! These are a perfect picnic pairing.

SO-GOOD BROWNIES (page 228) Your tailgaters will be cheering "Go chocolate!" when you serve up these decadent delights.

The 10 Commandments of College Football Fandom

There's an old saying that in the South, football is religion, and every Saturday is a holy day. So we compiled these inscribed-in-pigskin imperatives for game day.

COMMANDMENT 2: Thou shalt mind your manners and act with class. This is, after all, just a game!

COMMANDMENT 1: Thou shalt wear team colors. But think twice before adorning yourself with body paint—you don't want to be the Internet photo that goes viral.

COMMANDMENT 5: Thou shalt support the coach. He's the boss!

COMMANDMENT 3: Thou shalt be respectful to visiting teams. Remember: Southern ladies and gentlemen shouldn't boo.

COMMANDMENT 4: Thou shalt know—and sing— your team's fight song from beginning to end. Sure, you can "watermelon watermelon" your way through the alma mater, but not memorizing the fight song is a fan failure.

COMMANDMENT 6: **Thou shalt set up a tailgate no fewer than three hours before kickoff (six if it's a night game).** Table linens and matching koozies encouraged, but not required.

COMMANDMENT 7: **Thou shalt stay through the fourth quarter—rain or shine.** That's what ponchos are for, y'all.

COMMANDMENT 9: **Thou shalt respect the solemnity of game day** by planning weddings, births, and other life events around the football schedule.

COMMANDMENT 8: **Thou shalt theme your tailgate food around the visiting rival.** But be nice. You will play them again next year!

COMMANDMENT 10: **Thou shalt not covet other teams' bowl games, national championships, or Heisman Trophy wins.** There's always next year.

Cinnamon-Pecan Rolls,
page 32

(2)

EARLY MORNING WARM-UPS

Saturday morning in the South means eggs, grits, biscuits, and other breakfast and brunch favorites. These hearty dishes are a great start for a day full of fanfare and football.

Simple Grits with Toppings

MAKES: 8 servings | **HANDS-ON TIME:** 5 min. | **TOTAL TIME:** 18 min.

2	tsp. salt	**Toppings:** hot sauce, sliced green
2	cups uncooked quick-cooking grits	onions, chopped tomatoes, cooked and crumbled bacon, Fried Chicken
6	Tbsp. butter	Bites (page 85), shredded Gouda
½	tsp. pepper	cheese, shredded Cheddar cheese

1. Bring salt and 8 cups water to a boil in a Dutch oven over medium-high heat.
2. Whisk in grits, reduce heat to low, and cook, stirring occasionally, 8 minutes or until creamy.
3. Whisk in butter and pepper. Transfer to a slow cooker to keep warm, and serve with desired toppings.

Fruit Salad with Yogurt

MAKES: 8 servings | **HANDS-ON TIME:** 10 min. | **TOTAL TIME:** 10 min.

4	cups fresh pineapple chunks	2	cups Greek yogurt
1	qt. strawberries, halved	1	Tbsp. dark brown sugar
3	cups seedless green grapes	1	Tbsp. honey
2	mangoes, peeled and sliced		
2	(4-oz.) containers fresh raspberries		

1. Toss together first 5 ingredients in a large serving bowl. Spoon yogurt into a separate serving bowl; sprinkle yogurt with sugar, and drizzle with honey.

Creamy Grits Casserole

MAKES: 8 servings | **HANDS-ON TIME:** 10 min. | **TOTAL TIME:** 55 min.

1¼	cups uncooked regular grits	1	(10-oz.) block sharp Cheddar cheese, shredded
2	cups chicken broth		
2	cups milk	1	(4-oz.) smoked Gouda cheese round, shredded
1	tsp. salt		
¼	tsp. ground red pepper	2	large eggs, lightly beaten
½	cup butter, cut into cubes		

1. Preheat oven to 350°. Bring grits, chicken broth, and next 3 ingredients to a boil in a medium saucepan over medium-high heat; reduce heat to low, and simmer, stirring occasionally, 4 to 5 minutes or until thickened. Stir in butter and cheeses until melted.
2. Gradually stir about one-fourth hot grits mixture into eggs; add egg mixture to remaining hot grits mixture, stirring constantly. Pour grits mixture into a lightly greased 2½-qt. baking dish.
3. Bake at 350° for 35 to 40 minutes or until golden brown and edges are bubbly. Let stand 5 minutes before serving.

Serve with pork tenderloin or grilled rib eyes for a company-worthy supper.

Simple Grits with Toppings

Scrambled Egg Muffin
Sliders

Scrambled Egg Muffin Sliders

MAKES: 1 dozen | **HANDS-ON TIME:** 30 min. | **TOTAL TIME:** 55 min.

6	bacon slices
2	cups self-rising white cornmeal mix
1	Tbsp. sugar
1½	cups buttermilk
1	large egg
4	Tbsp. butter, melted

1	cup (4 oz.) shredded sharp Cheddar cheese
	Vegetable cooking spray
8	large eggs
½	tsp. Creole seasoning
1	Tbsp. butter

1. Preheat oven to 425°. Cook bacon in a large skillet over medium-high heat 12 to 14 minutes or until crisp; remove bacon, and drain on paper towels. Crumble bacon.

2. Heat a 12-cup muffin pan in oven 5 minutes.

3. Meanwhile, combine cornmeal mix and sugar in a medium bowl; make a well in center of mixture.

4. Stir together buttermilk and egg; add to cornmeal mixture, stirring just until dry ingredients are moistened. Stir in melted butter, cheese, and bacon. Remove pan from oven, and coat with cooking spray. Spoon batter into hot muffin pan, filling almost completely full.

5. Bake at 425° for 15 to 20 minutes or until golden. Remove from pan to a wire rack, and let cool 10 minutes.

6. Whisk together eggs, 1 Tbsp. water, and Creole seasoning in a medium bowl. Melt 1 Tbsp. butter in a large nonstick skillet. Add egg mixture, and cook, without stirring, 2 to 3 minutes or until eggs begin to set on bottom. Gently draw cooked edges away from sides of skillet to form large pieces. Cook, stirring occasionally, 4 to 5 minutes or until eggs are thickened and moist. (Do not overstir.) Cut muffins in half, and spoon eggs over bottom halves. Cover with top halves of muffins.

Note: We tested with White Lily White Cornmeal Mix.

Sausage-Hash Brown Breakfast Casserole

MAKES: 10 servings | **HANDS-ON TIME:** 20 min. | **TOTAL TIME:** 55 min.

1	lb. mild ground pork sausage
1	lb. hot ground pork sausage
1	(30-oz.) package frozen hash browns
½	tsp. pepper

1½	tsp. salt, divided
1	cup (4 oz.) shredded Cheddar cheese
6	large eggs
2	cups milk

1. Preheat oven to 350°. Cook sausages in a large skillet over medium-high heat, stirring often, 8 minutes or until sausage crumbles and is no longer pink. Drain well.

2. Prepare hash browns according to package directions, using pepper and ½ tsp. salt.

3. Stir together hash browns, sausage, and cheese. Pour into a lightly greased 13- x 9-inch baking dish.

4. Whisk together eggs, milk, and remaining 1 tsp. salt. Pour over potato mixture.

5. Bake at 350° for 35 to 40 minutes or until set.

Prepare muffins one day before the game if traveling out of town, and reheat in the microwave for a few seconds until warm. Meanwhile, cook the eggs for an even faster breakfast before you go-go-go!

Team allegiance kicks in early with a young Alabama fan.

SWEET HOME
Alabama

This is holy ground.
Scholars think here. Students play here. Fans gather here.
Yesterday, today, tomorrow—the Quad was and always will be the heart of
The University of Alabama®.

In 1831, Tuscaloosa was an untamed outpost on the western frontier of a brand-new state. Pioneers carved a square of grass out of the wilderness and built a school around it. Remains of the original campus lie just beneath the Quad. Bama's earliest gridiron battles were fought here too.

These days, the 22-acre Quad hosts a huge lawn party on game day. Even those not lucky enough to tailgate here stroll through and pay homage. At Denny Chimes, prints of past football captains are enshrined in the Walk of Fame. Bama's Million Dollar Band assembles at the Gorgas Library to serenade the crowd before marching across the Quad to the stadium.

At Bryant-Denny Stadium, football is played in the shadow of legendary coach Paul "Bear" Bryant. His acclaimed black-and-white houndstooth-print hat has created a fashion statement that's nearly as ubiquitous as crimson and white. A pep talk from Bear, broadcast before the team runs onto the field, drives the crowd wild.

Yet winning is Alabama's most enduring football legacy, and it has been since the Crimson Tide took its first national title in 1925. Game-day gatherings at the Quad are simply celebrations of the school's winning ways. "The Quad is the most beautiful place on the planet," declares one alum. "It never loses its magic."

Numbers first appeared on Alabama's helmets in 1957, then a common practice for many schools. Today, it's the only major college program that carries on the tradition.

Tuscaloosa, AL

A trip to Tuscaloosa is not complete without a visit to Dreamland.

Not much has changed since Dreamland first opened more than 50 years ago.

The bronze bells of Denny Chimes mark the hour at The University of Alabama, causing the students strolling across the Tuscaloosa campus to pick up their pace. "You never have to wear a watch on campus," says Montgomery lawyer Clint Daughtrey. "When you hear the chimes, you know it's either the hour or the quarter hour."

Named for a former university president, the 115-foot tower anchors the south side of the Quad, a stretch of green at the center of the campus. Like generations before him, Clint came here as a student and returns as a loyal alum.

"In some ways, it feels like I never left," he says. "You can walk across campus and pass the President's Mansion, which was one of the only buildings on campus the Union soldiers didn't burn. Then there are new buildings, such as Shelby Hall, that opened after I graduated. It seems like a contradiction, but it's really more of an evolution."

Though Tuscaloosa and the university have evolved together, the town remains relatively small and manageable—except on game days. T-town's population more than doubles when the Tide plays at home, causing residents and fans to make adjustments. "Driving on game day is a thing of the past," Clint admits. "It's best to find a place to park and plan to walk for the rest of the day."

Historical Hot Spot

Football fans of any stripe will want to stop by the **Paul W. Bryant Museum.** Displays feature highlights from every Bama season, from 1892 through the present. There's a wide array of U of A memorabilia as well as a Waterford crystal replica of Bear Bryant's houndstooth hat. Researchers from around the country come here to study the sport of college football and the vast Alabama football video archives.

Quintessential Food Finds

For many, a trip to Tuscaloosa demands a pilgrimage to the original **Dreamland Bar-B-Que.** Sausage has joined slow-cooked ribs on the menu, and there are now three sides from which to choose, but the barbecue is still served with Big Daddy's famous sauce and white bread for dipping. "I'll eat at the franchises, but I won't eat ribs at any Dreamland other than the one off Jug Factory Road in Jerusalem Heights in Tuscaloosa, Alabama," Clint states emphatically. "It just seems blasphemous to do so."

Also an institution in these parts, **City Cafe** sits just across the Black Warrior River in Northport. This traditional meat 'n' three serves

Denny Chimes

heaping helpings of fried chicken, mac and cheese, okra, turnip greens, and fried green tomatoes. At peak times, it's not unusual for patrons who are waiting to hover over those who are sitting, particularly if plates are empty. Connoisseurs say the ribs from **Archibald's Bar-B-Q** in Northport rival Dreamland's—without the wait.

The Houndstooth Sports Bar anchors The Strip, the section of

University Boulevard closest to campus. Flat-screen TVs hang in every corner, even the bathrooms, so patrons won't miss a second of the action. From Friday lunch through Saturday night (when the Tide is playing at home), **Big Bad Wolves BBQ** sets up on the front steps of The Houndstooth to sell its coveted pulled pork barbecue nachos drizzled with sweet sauce and nacho cheese. There's no sign for **Gallette's,** but most students can point the way. Fans favor the Yellow Hammer, an adult libation named for the state bird and Bama's famous end-of-game chant.

As University Boulevard continues, it cuts straight through the downtown business district. **DePalma's** serves brick-oven pizza, while **Innisfree Irish Pub** is famous for fried pickles and cold beer. **FIVE** has a fine-dining menu built around its signature number, but it also boasts a Sunday brunch with waffles and wings, a Bloody Mary bar, and mimosas. "Downtown Tuscaloosa becomes an extension of campus and tailgating on a game day," Clint explains.

For more information: **Tuscaloosa Tourism and Sports Commission, 800/538-8696** or **205/391-9200.**

Paul "Bear" Bryant

Innisfree Irish Pub

Alabama Crimson Tide® Menu

Fruit Salad with Yogurt (page 22)

Simple Grits with Toppings (page 22)

Fried Chicken Bites (page 85)
or Parmesan-Pecan Fried Chicken
(page 169)

Roll Tide® Breakfast Rolls
(recipe below)

Coffee Cake Pound Cake (page 38)

Time out! Go leaner and make a substitution— 1½ cups egg substitute for eggs and reduced-fat pork sausage for sausage.

Roll Tide Breakfast Rolls

MAKES: 10 servings | **HANDS-ON TIME:** 20 min. | **TOTAL TIME:** 20 min.

10   (6-inch) fajita-size flour tortillas
½   (16-oz.) package ground pork sausage
6   large eggs
Vegetable cooking spray
½   cup shredded colby-Jack cheese blend
Salsa (optional)
Sour cream (optional)

1. Preheat oven to 250°. Wrap tortillas loosely with aluminum foil, and place in oven 10 minutes.

2. Meanwhile, cook sausage in a large skillet over medium-high heat, stirring often, 8 minutes or until sausage crumbles and is no longer pink; drain. Remove sausage from skillet, and pat dry with paper towels. Wipe skillet clean. Reduce heat to medium.

3. Whisk together eggs and 2 Tbsp. water. Coat same skillet with cooking spray; add egg mixture, and cook, without stirring, 2 to 3 minutes or until eggs begin to set on bottom. Gently draw cooked edges away from sides of skillet to form large pieces. Cook, stirring occasionally, 2 minutes or until eggs are thickened but still moist. (Do not overstir.)

4. Spoon sausage and eggs onto tortillas, and sprinkle with cheese; roll up tortillas. Serve with salsa and sour cream, if desired.

Sausage Balls

MAKES: about 8 dozen | **HANDS-ON TIME:** 10 min. | **TOTAL TIME:** 25 min.

3	cups all-purpose baking mix	1	(10-oz.) block sharp Cheddar
1	lb. hot ground pork sausage		cheese, shredded

1. Preheat oven to 400°. Combine all ingredients in a large bowl, pressing mixture together with hands. Shape into ¾-inch balls, and place on lightly greased baking sheets.

2. Bake at 400° for 15 to 18 minutes or until lightly browned.

Note: We tested with Cracker Barrel Sharp Cheddar Cheese.

Use freshly shredded cheese for these sausage balls—a traditional Southern favorite.

Ambrosia

MAKES: 8 to 10 servings | **HANDS-ON TIME:** 30 min. | **TOTAL TIME:** 2 hr., 30 min.

12	navel oranges, peeled and sectioned	2	Tbsp. powdered sugar
1	fresh pineapple, peeled, cored, and cut into cubes	1	cup freshly grated coconut

1. Toss together fruit and powdered sugar in a large bowl.

2. Place one-third fruit mixture in a serving bowl. Top with one-third coconut. Repeat layers twice. Cover and chill 2 hours.

 Extra Point: For a twist, add three red grapefruit, peeled and sectioned, to the fruit mixture.

Simple enough for a rookie baker, this easy yeast roll dough rises in just 30 minutes. You'll be moving on from freshman to sophomore status with grace and ease.

Cinnamon-Pecan Rolls

MAKES: 12 rolls | **HANDS-ON TIME:** 20 min. | **TOTAL TIME:** 1 hr., 25 min.

1	cup chopped pecans	2	tsp. ground cinnamon
1	(16-oz.) package hot roll mix	1	cup powdered sugar
½	cup butter, softened	2	Tbsp. milk
1	cup firmly packed light brown sugar	1	tsp. vanilla extract

1. Preheat oven to 350°. Bake pecans in a single layer in a shallow pan 5 to 7 minutes or until toasted and fragrant, stirring halfway through.

2. Prepare hot roll dough according to package directions; let dough stand 5 minutes. Roll dough into a 15- x 10-inch rectangle; spread with softened butter. Stir together brown sugar and cinnamon; sprinkle over butter. Sprinkle pecans over brown sugar mixture. Roll up tightly, starting at 1 long end; cut into 12 slices. Place rolls, cut sides down, in a lightly greased 12-inch cast-iron skillet or 13- x 9-inch pan. Cover loosely with plastic wrap and a cloth towel; let rise in a warm place (85°), free from drafts, 30 minutes or until doubled in bulk.

3. Preheat oven to 375°. Uncover rolls, and bake 20 to 25 minutes or until center rolls are golden brown and done. Let cool in pan on a wire rack 10 minutes. Stir together powdered sugar, milk, and vanilla; drizzle over rolls.

Note: We tested with Pillsbury Specialty Mix Hot Roll Mix.

Cream Cheese-Banana-Nut Bread

MAKES: 2 loaves | **HANDS-ON TIME:** 15 min. | **TOTAL TIME:** 2 hr., 10 min.

1¼	cups chopped pecans, divided	½	tsp. baking powder
¼	cup butter, softened	½	tsp. baking soda
1	(8-oz.) package ⅓-less-fat cream cheese, softened	½	tsp. salt
		1	cup buttermilk
1	cup sugar	1½	cups mashed very ripe bananas (1¼ lb. unpeeled bananas, about 4 medium)
2	large eggs		
1½	cups whole wheat flour	½	tsp. vanilla extract
1½	cups all-purpose flour		

1. Preheat oven to 350°. Place ¾ cup pecans in a single layer on a baking sheet, and bake 12 to 15 minutes or until toasted and fragrant, stirring after 6 minutes.

2. Beat butter and cream cheese at medium speed with an electric mixer until creamy. Gradually add sugar, beating until light and fluffy. Add eggs, 1 at a time, beating just until blended after each addition.

3. Combine whole wheat flour and next 4 ingredients; gradually add to butter mixture alternately with buttermilk, beginning and ending with flour mixture. Beat at low speed just until blended after each addition. Stir in bananas, ¾ cup toasted pecans, and vanilla. Spoon batter into 2 greased and floured 8- x 4-inch loaf pans. Sprinkle with remaining ½ cup pecans.

4. Bake at 350° for 1 hour or until a long wooden pick inserted in center comes out clean and sides of bread pull away from pan, shielding with aluminum foil during last 15 minutes to prevent excessive browning, if necessary. Cool bread in pans on wire racks 10 minutes. Remove from pans to wire racks. Let cool 30 minutes.

> If you've never worked with whole wheat flour, accurate measuring is everything. Be sure to spoon the flour into a dry measuring cup (do not pack), and level it off with a straight edge.

Cream Cheese Scrambled Eggs

MAKES: 4 to 6 servings | **HANDS-ON TIME:** 10 min. | **TOTAL TIME:** 10 min.

8	large eggs	1	(3-oz.) package cream cheese, cut into cubes
¼	cup milk		
½	tsp. salt	⅓	cup chopped fresh basil (optional)
½	tsp. pepper		
1	Tbsp. butter		

1. Whisk together first 4 ingredients.

2. Melt butter in a large nonstick skillet over medium heat; add egg mixture, and cook, without stirring, 2 to 3 minutes or until eggs begin to set on bottom. Sprinkle cream cheese cubes over egg mixture; gently draw cooked eggs away from sides of skillet to form large pieces.

3. Cook, stirring occasionally, 2 minutes or until eggs are thickened and moist. (Do not overstir.) Remove from heat. Stir in chopped basil before serving, if desired.

On January 1, 1966, The University of Alabama cheerleaders celebrated as Bear Bryant's Tide prevailed over Nebraska in the Orange Bowl. It was the first-ever night bowl game.

Dried Cherry-Walnut Sweet Rolls

MAKES: about 2 dozen | **HANDS-ON TIME:** 10 min. | **TOTAL TIME:** 1 hr., 15 min.

1	**(25-oz.) package frozen roll dough, thawed according to package directions**	1	**(3-oz.) package dried cherries, chopped**
½	**cup chopped walnuts**	3	**Tbsp. granulated sugar**
¼	**cup butter, melted**	¾	**tsp. pumpkin pie spice**
		2	**cups powdered sugar**
		3	**Tbsp. hot water**

1. Preheat oven to 200°.

2. Place dough balls in 2 greased 9-inch round cake pans. Turn off oven. Cover dough balls with plastic wrap; let rise in oven 25 to 30 minutes or until doubled in bulk. Remove from oven. Remove and discard plastic wrap.

3. Preheat oven to 350°. Stir together walnuts and next 4 ingredients. Sprinkle mixture over dough in pans.

4. Bake at 350° for 12 to 15 minutes or until golden brown. Cool completely (about 30 minutes).

5. Stir together powdered sugar and 3 Tbsp. hot water. Drizzle over rolls.

Note: We tested with Rich's Enriched Homestyle Roll Dough.

Pecan-Golden Raisin Sweet Rolls: Substitute 1½ cups chopped pecans for walnuts, ½ cup golden raisins for cherries, ½ cup firmly packed dark brown sugar for granulated sugar, and ¾ tsp. apple pie spice for pumpkin pie spice. Proceed with recipe as directed.

Apricot-Orange Sweet Rolls: Reduce granulated sugar to 2 Tbsp. Substitute 1 (6-oz.) package dried apricots, chopped, for cherries; 1 Tbsp. orange zest for ¾ tsp. pumpkin pie spice; and 3 Tbsp. fresh orange juice for hot water. Proceed with recipe as directed.

Planning to park it in your jammies for the early morning game? Your family will be enjoying these long before the winners are predicted by, well, you know who...the guy wearing the mascot head.

Easy Orange Rolls

MAKES: 11 rolls | **HANDS-ON TIME:** 15 min. | **TOTAL TIME:** 40 min.

½	**(8-oz.) package cream cheese, softened**	2	**Tbsp. granulated sugar**
¼	**cup firmly packed light brown sugar**	1	**Tbsp. butter, melted**
1½	**tsp. orange zest**	½	**cup powdered sugar**
1	**(11-oz.) can refrigerated French bread dough**	1	**Tbsp. orange juice**

1. Preheat oven to 375°. Beat cream cheese, light brown sugar, and orange zest at medium speed with an electric mixer until smooth.

2. Unroll French bread dough onto a lightly floured surface. Spread cream cheese mixture over dough, leaving a ¼-inch border. Sprinkle with granulated sugar. Gently roll up dough, starting at 1 long side. Cut into 11 (1¼-inch) slices. Place slices in a lightly greased 8-inch round cake pan. Brush top of dough with melted butter. Bake at 375° for 25 to 30 minutes or until golden. Stir together powdered sugar and orange juice in a small bowl until smooth. Drizzle over hot rolls. Serve immediately.

Note: We tested with Pillsbury Crusty French Loaf.

Dried Cherry-Walnut
Sweet Rolls

This recipe is perfect for a road trip or if you plan to cheer from home. Make the day before the big game, cool completely, and wrap with aluminum foil.

Streusel Coffee Cake

MAKES: 8 to 10 servings | **HANDS-ON TIME:** 15 min. | **TOTAL TIME:** 1 hr., 15 min., including topping

- ½   **cup butter, softened**
- 1   **(8-oz.) package cream cheese, softened**
- 1¼   **cups sugar**
- 2   **large eggs**
- 2   **cups all-purpose flour**
- 2   **tsp. baking powder**
- ½   **tsp. baking soda**
- ½   **tsp. salt**
- ½   **cup milk**
- 1   **tsp. vanilla extract**
- ½   **tsp. almond extract**

Crumb Topping

1. Preheat oven to 350°. Beat butter and cream cheese at medium speed with an electric mixer until creamy. Gradually add sugar, beating at medium speed until light and fluffy. Add eggs, 1 at a time, beating just until blended.

2. Sift together flour and next 3 ingredients; add to butter mixture alternately with milk, beginning and ending with flour mixture. Beat at low speed just until blended after each addition. Stir in vanilla and almond extracts. Pour batter into a greased 13- x 9-inch pan; sprinkle with Crumb Topping.

3. Bake at 350° for 35 to 40 minutes or until a wooden pick inserted in center comes out clean. Let cool 20 minutes before serving.

Crumb Topping

MAKES: about 1¾ cups | **HANDS-ON TIME:** 5 min. | **TOTAL TIME:** 5 min.

- ½   **cup all-purpose flour**
- ½   **cup sugar**
- ½   **cup coarsely chopped pecans**
- ¼   **cup butter**

1. Stir together flour, sugar, and coarsely chopped pecans in a bowl. Cut in butter with a pastry blender or fork until mixture resembles small peas.

Streusel Coffee Cake

Coffee Cake Pound Cake

MAKES: 12 servings | **HANDS-ON TIME:** 30 min. | **TOTAL TIME:** 3 hr., 25 min.

PECAN STREUSEL
½ cup firmly packed brown sugar
½ cup all-purpose flour
1 tsp. ground cinnamon
¼ cup butter
¾ cup chopped pecans

POUND CAKE BATTER
1 cup finely chopped pecans
1 cup butter, softened

2½ cups granulated sugar
6 large eggs
3 cups all-purpose flour
¼ tsp. baking soda
1 (8-oz.) container sour cream
2 tsp. vanilla extract
¼ cup firmly packed brown sugar
1½ tsp. ground cinnamon

1. Prepare Pecan Streusel: Combine first 3 ingredients in a bowl. Cut in butter with a pastry blender or fork until mixture resembles small peas. Stir in ¾ cup pecans.

2. Prepare Pound Cake Batter: Preheat oven to 350°. Bake 1 cup pecans in a single layer in a shallow pan 5 to 7 minutes or until lightly toasted and fragrant, stirring halfway through. Cool 20 minutes. Reduce oven temperature to 325°.

3. Beat butter at medium speed with a heavy-duty electric stand mixer until creamy. Gradually add granulated sugar, beating until light and fluffy. Add eggs, 1 at a time, beating just until yellow disappears.

4. Stir together flour and baking soda; add to butter mixture alternately with sour cream, beginning and ending with flour mixture. Beat at low speed just until blended after each addition. Stir in vanilla.

5. Pour half of batter into a greased and floured 10-inch (12-cup) tube pan. Stir together toasted pecans, brown sugar, and cinnamon; sprinkle over batter. Spoon remaining batter over pecan mixture; sprinkle with Pecan Streusel.

6. Bake at 325° for 1 hour and 20 minutes to 1 hour and 30 minutes or until a long wooden pick inserted in center comes out clean. Cool in pan on a wire rack 10 to 15 minutes; remove from pan to wire rack, and cool completely (about 1 hour).

Citrus-Vanilla Bean Marmalade

MAKES: about 2 cups | **HANDS-ON TIME:** 20 min. | **TOTAL TIME:** 2 hr., 15 min., plus 1 day for chilling

1 vanilla bean
2 large Valencia or navel oranges
2 medium-size red grapefruit

1 lemon
2 cups sugar
⅛ tsp. kosher salt

1. Split vanilla bean lengthwise, and scrape out seeds.

2. Grate zest from oranges to equal 1 Tbsp. Repeat with grapefruit. Grate zest from lemon to equal 1 tsp.

3. Peel and section oranges, grapefruit, and lemon, holding fruit over a bowl to collect juices.

4. Stir together vanilla bean and seeds; orange, grapefruit, and lemon zest; fruit segments; sugar; kosher salt; ⅓ cup fruit juices; and 1¾ cups water in a large saucepan; bring to a boil. Reduce heat, and simmer, stirring occasionally, 50 minutes or until a candy thermometer registers 225° and mixture is slightly thickened. Cool completely (about 1 hour; mixture will thicken as it cools). Discard vanilla bean; pour marmalade into 2 (8-oz.) jars or airtight containers, and chill 24 hours. Store marmalade in refrigerator up to 3 weeks.

Expect a sweeter, less bitter marmalade than what's commonly sold. While Auburn, Florida, and Tennessee fans will praise it for its orange hue, any true Southerner will appreciate its fresh flavor atop biscuits or breakfast bread.

Coffee Cake Pound Cake

CALLING

The Hogs™

It begins with a single fan. He stands, raises his arms in the air, fingers wiggling, and begins a high-pitched "Wooo!" First one, then another, they join in, until soon every Arkansas® fan in Donald W. Reynolds Razorback® Stadium rises as one to Call the Hogs™.

"Wooo, Pig! Sooie!" Three times. Arms come down on "Pig," fists pump the air on "Sooie" and then there's the finish: "Razorbacks"—thus concluding the Hog Call. When the score is close, fans Call the Hogs. When Lady Luck takes a hike, they Call the Hogs. When victory is secure, they Call the Hogs. It's an eerie sound, to be sure, chilling to outsiders, but thrilling to Razorback fans around the globe.

The University of Arkansas adopted its feral porcine mascot in 1910 after an impromptu speech by then-coach Hugo Bezdek. His gritty 1909 team outscored opponents 186-18 on the way to an undefeated season. After the LSU game, Bezdek said his team played like a "wild band of razorback hogs." U of A teams still wear Cardinal red, but a 1910 student vote blessed the nickname Razorbacks.

Pork barbecue is a staple at Arkansas tailgates, and Herman's Ribhouse is the go-to restaurant after a game—or anytime you're in Fayetteville. Of course, many wonder how U of A acolytes can stomach the idea of feasting on the thing they love most. It's not such a leap, says one carnivorous alum. "You are what you eat."

Hog fans often own and wear Hog Hats, red plastic toppers fashioned in the shape of a running Razorback. But the true identifying mark of an Arkansas fan is the Hog Call. Whether in a stadium or in a church, fans Call the Hogs whenever and wherever they gather.

The Arkansas faithful Call
the Hogs on game day—
Wooo, Pig! Sooie!

Fayetteville, AR

Begun by the class of 1905, Senior Walk now lists the names of more than 120,000 graduates.

The names on the slabs comprising Senior Walk were stamped by hand until 1986, when university Physical Plant employees invented the Sand Hog, a machine whose purpose is to etch the names in Senior Walk.

A young co-ed and her mother walk slowly along the sidewalk on campus at the University of Arkansas, arms linked and heads bent in concentration as they study the ground. "There it is, Mom!" the girl exclaims suddenly. "There's your name."

It's not unusual, especially on game days when the campus is crowded, to find people wandering around and staring at the ground. Every Arkansas graduate's name is etched into the Senior Walk here, with names starting at the steps of Old Main and stretching for 5 miles across campus. "There are famous graduates and not so famous, but everyone gets to live forever on the sidewalks here," says alumnus Art Meripol. "I am there, and right next to me is my brother Paul. Very cool!"

Campus Charmers

The chimes on the oldest building on campus, **Old Main**, ring each hour from 8 a.m. to 8 p.m. and play the university's alma mater at 5 p.m. every day. Old Main also anchors the University of Arkansas Campus Historic District, which encompasses 25 buildings including 15 historic structures that once formed the core of campus. The Historic District also boasts an arboretum that contains a large variety of trees.

Instead of demolishing **Carnall Hall,** the former residence hall near Old Main, trustees transformed it into a hotel and restaurant. Though now privately owned, the facility is used to train students majoring in hospitality and restaurant management. The inn boasts 49 rooms, no two alike, and **Ella's Restaurant** is a fine-dining gem. Many locals say it serves the city's best Sunday brunch.

Entertainment District Delights

Dickson Street, known locally as The Drag, serves as the city's entertainment district. Long a local favorite, **Bordinos** features a Northern Italian menu that changes seasonally, fine wines, and live music. Lunch is a

treat, plus there's a three-course first seating menu and a reservations-only Chef's Table. **Common Grounds**, a gourmet espresso bar, offers fresh-baked pastries, sandwiches, and a full bar. Not only does **Hog Haus Brewing Company** serve excellent craft beers and pub food, it also sells Growlers To Go, half-gallon jars of their own ales.

Soul Food

Just a block north of the square, **Hugo's** remains a favorite for cooked-to-order specialty burgers including the popular Bleu Moon. **Momma Dean's** feeds the soul with chicken and dumplings, butter beans, and collard greens. Don't miss Momma's signature dish—Twice Cooked Chicken that's first cooked, then fried, to a golden brown.

Still, **Herman's Ribhouse** remains the all-time favorite for Razorback fans. Celebrity photos and sports memorabilia line the paneled walls, and checkered tablecloths and curtains echo the school's red-and-white colors. Hungry customers nibble on saltine crackers and homemade salsa while they wait for pork ribs and hand-cut steaks to come off the grill. There's even a deck out back with live music and outdoor dining.

For the best fine dining in Northwest Arkansas, food lovers reserve a table at **James at the Mill,** just 3 miles north of town in tiny Johnson, Arkansas. This sophisticated restaurant adjoins a restored 1835 gristmill that now houses a charming 48-room inn. Chef Miles James serves what he calls Ozark Plateau Cuisine, which features regional cooking styles and fresh, local ingredients. Innovative dishes range from homemade andouille sausage corn dogs to hickory smoked bone-in rib eyes rubbed with adobo sauce.

For the History Buffs

Presidential history fans will want to stop by the **Clinton House Museum**, where the former president and first lady, Bill and Hillary Clinton, lived while in Fayetteville. The power couple married in the living room of this modest bungalow, and exhibits focus on the genesis of their political careers.

Francophiles should plan a shopping excursion too. Two shops— **French Metro Antiques** on Dickson and **French Quarters Antiques** on North Block—offer the finest imported French furniture and accessories, as well as some of the best prices.

Perhaps the most impressive development in the Ozarks in recent years is the November 2011 opening of the **Crystal Bridges Museum of American Art** in nearby Bentonville. Funded by Walmart heiress Alice Walton, the museum features a vast permanent collection, from Colonial portraits to modern works. The glass-and-wood building set among 120 acres of forest and designed by Moshie Safdie is itself a work of art. Best of all, admission is free.

For more information: **Fayetteville Visitors Bureau, 800/766-4626** or **479/521-5776.**

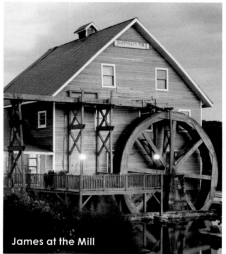

James at the Mill

Crystal Bridges Museum of American Art

Arkansas Razorbacks® Menu

Coffee Milk Punch (page 48)

Ambrosia (page 32)

Cream Cheese Scrambled Eggs (page 33)

Sausage-Hash Brown Breakfast Casserole (page 25)

Wooo Pig Sooie™ Ham-Stuffed Biscuits with Mustard Butter (recipe below)

Cinnamon-Pecan Rolls (page 32)

Ham and biscuits are popular at tailgates across the South—including Fayetteville. Use your favorite sliced, baked ham to stuff into these soft biscuits, and slather with plenty of Mustard Butter.

Wooo Pig Sooie Ham-Stuffed Biscuits with Mustard Butter

MAKES: 5 dozen | **HANDS-ON TIME:** 1 hr. | **TOTAL TIME:** 2 hr., including butter

1	(¼-oz.) envelope active dry yeast	1½	Tbsp. baking powder
½	cup warm water (100° to 110°)	1½	tsp. salt
2	cups buttermilk	½	tsp. baking soda
5½	cups all-purpose flour	¾	cup shortening
¼	cup sugar		Mustard Butter (page 205)
		2	lb. thinly sliced cooked ham

1. Combine yeast and ½ cup warm water in a 4-cup liquid measuring cup, and let mixture stand 5 minutes. Stir in buttermilk.

2. Combine flour and next 4 ingredients in a large bowl; cut in shortening with a pastry blender or fork until mixture resembles small peas and mixture is crumbly. Add buttermilk mixture, stirring with a fork just until dry ingredients are moistened.

3. Turn dough out onto a well-floured surface, and knead 4 or 5 times.

4. Roll dough to ½-inch thickness; cut with a 2-inch round cutter, and place on lightly greased baking sheets. Cover and let rise in a warm place (85°), free from drafts, 1 hour.

5. Preheat oven to 425°. Bake for 10 to 12 minutes or until golden. Split each biscuit, and spread with Mustard Butter. Stuff biscuits with ham.

Homemade Limeade,
page 58

(3)
CHEERS

Here's to a season full of reasons to toast the team. This array of beverages—from warm ciders and cocoas to refreshing sippers and punch—gives plenty of options.

> "The morning has to start with massive amounts of coffee straight from the ol' Gator coffee mug! Then it's time to put on the lucky Gator T-shirt. Every year we all go out and get a *new* lucky T-shirt for that season. Gotta have it on all day long for game days."
>
> —SISTER HAZEL, Gainesville, Florida-bred band and Gator fans, on game-day superstitions

UF mascots give a big "Go Gators" at Ben Hill Griffin Stadium.

Rich 'n' Thick Hot Chocolate

MAKES: about 4 cups | **HANDS-ON TIME:** 15 min. | **TOTAL TIME:** 15 min.

- 2 tsp. cornstarch
- 4 cups milk, divided
- 2 (3.5-oz.) dark chocolate bars (at least 70% cacao), chopped
- ⅓ cup honey
- 1 tsp. vanilla extract
- Pinch of salt
- Garnish: jumbo marshmallows

1. Whisk together cornstarch and ½ cup milk until smooth.

2. Cook remaining 3½ cups milk in a large nonaluminum saucepan over medium heat until bubbles appear around edge of saucepan (about 4 minutes; do not boil). Whisk in chocolate, honey, vanilla, and salt until blended and smooth. Whisk in cornstarch mixture.

3. Bring milk mixture to a light boil, whisking frequently (about 4 minutes). Remove from heat. Let cool slightly. (Mixture will thicken as it cools.)

Note: We tested with Ghirardelli Intense Dark Twilight Delight 72% Cacao dark chocolate bar.

Mexican Rich 'n' Thick Hot Chocolate: Prepare recipe as directed through Step 2, whisking in 1¼ tsp. ground cinnamon and 1 tsp. ancho chile powder with chocolate. Proceed with recipe as directed.

Coffee Milk Punch

MAKES: about 9 cups | **HANDS-ON TIME:** 5 min. | **TOTAL TIME:** 1 hr.,10 min.

- 7 cups strong brewed hot coffee
- ½ cup hot fudge topping
- ¼ cup sugar
- 2 cups half-and-half
- 1 Tbsp. vanilla extract

1. Whisk together hot coffee, fudge topping, and sugar in a large Dutch oven until smooth. Add half-and-half and vanilla, stirring until blended. Bring mixture to a simmer over medium-high heat. Serve immediately. To serve cool, cover and chill 1 to 24 hours, and serve over ice.

 Extra Point: Pour punch into ice cube trays, wrap with aluminum foil, and insert small wooden craft sticks before freezing for a refreshing pop.

Rich 'n' Thick Hot
Chocolate

Touchdown Auburn! An AU cheerleader carries a flag to the end zone in celebration after a touchdown against the Arkansas Razorbacks.

Winner's Wassail

MAKES: 13 cups | **HANDS-ON TIME:** 15 min. | **TOTAL TIME:** 35 min.

2	tsp. whole allspice
2	tsp. whole cloves
6	cinnamon sticks

Cheesecloth

2	qt. apple cider
2	cups sugar
2	cups orange juice
1½	cups fresh lemon juice (about 13 lemons)

Garnish: fresh orange slices

1. Tie first 3 ingredients together in a piece of cheesecloth or coffee filter.

2. Bring cider and sugar to a boil in a large saucepan. Add spice bag; reduce heat, and simmer, covered, 10 minutes. Remove spice bag; discard.

3. Stir in orange juice, lemon juice, and 1 cup water; simmer 5 minutes or until heated. Serve hot.

Warm Citrus Cider

MAKES: about 4½ qt. | **HANDS-ON TIME:** 20 min. | **TOTAL TIME:** 30 min.

1	gal. apple cider
2	cups orange juice
½	cup fresh lemon juice
1	orange, sliced
1	lemon, sliced
1½	tsp. whole cloves
3	cinnamon sticks

1. Bring all ingredients to a boil in a saucepan. Reduce heat; simmer 10 minutes. Pour through a wire-mesh strainer into a pitcher; discard solids. Serve hot.

Southern sweet tea is known as the house wine of the South. Save precious minutes the day of the game and make this up to 2 days ahead of time.

Southern Sweet Tea

MAKES: 10 cups | **HANDS-ON TIME:** 5 min. | **TOTAL TIME:** 20 min.

3	cups water
2	family-size tea bags
¾	cup sugar
6	cups cold water

1. Bring 3 cups water to a boil in a saucepan; add tea bags. Boil 1 minute; remove from heat. Cover and steep 10 minutes.

2. Discard tea bags. Add sugar, stirring until dissolved. Pour into a 1-gal. container, and add 6 cups cold water. Serve over ice.

 Extra Point: For added flavor in each glass, freeze tea in ice cube trays, and add to glass. Tea-flavored ice cubes are also delicious in lemonade.

Winner's Wassail

WHERE THE
Eagle Flies

A ripple of excitement races through
the crowd at Jordan-Hare as Nova—
a majestic golden eagle—leaps
off the upper balcony and circles
the stadium, soaring in the warm autumn
breeze. Then, the chant begins.
"Waaaaaar. . ."

The crowd screams in unison as the eagle drops out of the sky and lands near
midfield. "War, Eagle! Hey!" It's game time in Auburn, Alabama.

Nova's flight caps a sizzling pregame celebration that's second to none in
college football. Tailgating begins as early as Wednesday before kickoff in this,
the "loveliest village of the plain." By the time game day dawns, the AU campus
resembles a tent city with Tiger lovers occupying every piece of real estate, grass,
or asphalt as far as the eye can see.

While there's no official start time for tailgating, there is an absolute end—
diehard fans get to the stadium in time to see the eagle fly. "When I see that
golden-brown body streaking above the sea of orange and blue, I get a huge lump
in my throat," declares one teary alum. "There are just no words to explain the
pride I feel."

When the battle is over and Auburn prevails, excited Tiger fans
exit the stadium and race to Toomer's Corner to roll the century-old
trees flanking the university's entrance. The party's not over until
white tissue paper rains from the mighty oaks.

Before every home football game, one of Auburn's eagles circles the stadium and lands at midfield as an unwavering icon of the school's heroic spirit.

Auburn, AL

"When I think of Auburn, I think of Toomer's Corner."

After every football win, Auburn students and fans roll the old oaks at Toomer's Corner with toilet paper.

I n my mind, I see those magnificent live oak trees at Toomer's Corner guarding the university's oldest entrance at the intersection of Magnolia and College," alumna Jane Smith-Stage reminisces. "That's the heart of Auburn—the city and the university."

Catty-cornered across the street at Toomer's Drugs, which opened in 1896, customers belly up to the lunch counter for fresh-squeezed lemonade and grilled cheese sandwiches. Though the owners no longer fill prescriptions, the black-and-white tile floor announces, as it always has, "Welcome to Toomer's Corner." See the next page for the inside scoop on all the fan-favorite spots.

An Auburn Institution

Momma Goldberg's Deli boasts franchises all over the state, but the original still stands on the corner of Magnolia and Donahue in Auburn. Hungry students devour huge hoagies such as the famous Momma's Love, loaded with beef, ham, smoked turkey, Muenster cheese, and Momma's sauce. "It's an Auburn institution," Jane says.

Matchless Music Venue

A popular Auburn hot spot is **The War Eagle Supper Club**—a smoky dive bar where the motto is "cold beer, hot rock." First timers stand in line for a so-called membership, but it's the top place in the city for live music. Best of all, the Shot Bus picks partiers up and drops them off again so they don't have to drive. "My child went to the same places that I went growing up, and his child will go to the same places he did," Jane notes. "I love that!"

Top Attractions

Tiger sports fans love the **Jonathan Bell Lovelace Museum and Hall of Honor,** located inside Auburn Arena. Awash in orange and blue, the interactive museum holds Bo Jackson's Heisman Trophy and his retired No. 34 jersey as well as loads of other memorabilia. Fans can walk down memory lane, reliving highlights from every Tiger sport.

Auburn and nearby Opelika share the **Grand National**, 54 superb holes of golf that hug the shores of Lake Saugahatchee. Part of Alabama's renowned Robert Trent Jones Golf Trail, it's widely considered one of the top public courses in the country— and one of the most affordable. The full-service **Marriott Conference Center** overlooking the golf course offers the best lodging for miles around.

Auburn's population has grown to a little more than 53,000, and together with neighboring Opelika, it makes up one of the fastest growing metro areas in the country. It seems others are discovering what residents have always known: Auburn is a lovely place to live.

"There's a reason Auburn was tagged the 'loveliest village of the plain'," Jane says. "It is a very scenic, very pretty little town."

For more information: **Auburn & Opelika Tourism Bureau, 866/880-8747** or **334/887-8747.**

Robert Trent Jones Golf Trail at Grand National in Opelika, Alabama

Toomer's Drugs

Jonathan Bell Lovelace Museum

Auburn Tigers® Menu

Vanilla-Rosemary Lemonade
(recipe below)

Sausage, Bean, and Spinach Dip (page 93)

Slow-Cooked BBQ Chicken Sandwiches
(page 166)

Sweet Potato Cornbread (page 167)

Pickled Peppers and Onions (page 166)

Simple Slaw (page 167)

Lemonade Pie (page 244)

> "I think the Iron Bowl is the greatest rivalry in sports with the most passionate fans anywhere."
>
> —BRANDON COX, former Auburn quarterback

Vanilla-Rosemary Lemonade

MAKES: 6 cups | **HANDS-ON TIME:** 15 min. | **TOTAL TIME:** 3 hr., 45 min.

1½ cups sugar
1   vanilla bean, split
3   small fresh rosemary sprigs
3   cups fresh lemon juice (about 26 to 30 lemons)*
Garnishes: fresh rosemary sprigs, lemon slices

1. Combine sugar, vanilla bean, rosemary sprigs, and 3 cups water in a medium saucepan. Bring to a light boil over medium heat, stirring occasionally. Simmer 5 minutes. Remove from heat, and let cool 30 minutes. Pour through a fine wire-mesh strainer into a large pitcher, discarding solids. Stir in fresh lemon juice. Cover and chill 3 to 48 hours. Stir just before serving over ice.
* 3 (7.5-oz.) containers frozen lemon juice, thawed, may be substituted.

Fizzy Strawberry Lemonade

MAKES: about 7 cups | **HANDS-ON TIME:** 10 min. | **TOTAL TIME:** 10 min.

1   **(12-oz.) can frozen lemonade concentrate, thawed**
1   **(10-oz.) package frozen strawberries, partially thawed**
3   **Tbsp. sugar**
1   **(1-liter) bottle club soda, chilled**

1. Process first 3 ingredients in a blender until smooth, stopping to scrape down sides.
2. Pour strawberry mixture through a wire-mesh strainer into a large pitcher, discarding seeds; stir in club soda. Serve over ice.

Homemade Limeade

MAKES: about 8 cups | **HANDS-ON TIME:** 10 min. | **TOTAL TIME:** 8 hr., 10 min.

1½   **cups sugar**
½   **cup boiling water**
2   **tsp. lime zest**
1½   **cups fresh lime juice**
5   **cups cold water**

1. Stir together sugar and ½ cup boiling water until sugar dissolves.
2. Stir in lime zest, lime juice, and 5 cups cold water. Chill 8 hours.

Sweet Mint Tea

MAKES: 3 cups | **HANDS-ON TIME:** 10 min. | **TOTAL TIME:** 10 min.

½   **cup loosely packed fresh mint leaves**
1   **lemon, sliced**
2   **Tbsp. turbinado sugar**
3   **cups cold sweetened tea**
Crushed ice
Garnish: fresh mint sprigs

1. Combine first 3 ingredients in a 1-qt. pitcher. Press mint leaves against sides of pitcher with back of spoon to release flavors. Stir in tea. Serve over crushed ice.

Using store-bought sweetened tea saves time.

Berry Splash

MAKES: about 2 qt. | **HANDS-ON TIME:** 5 min. | **TOTAL TIME:** 5 min.

1   **(0.13-oz.) package unsweetened cherry drink mix**
6   **cups white cranberry juice**
¼   **cup sugar**
Garnish: fresh mint sprigs or strawberry leaves, frozen blueberry ice cubes

1. Stir together first 3 ingredients and 2 cups water in a large pitcher until sugar is dissolved. Cover and chill.
Note: We tested with Kool-Aid Cherry Unsweetened Soft Drink Mix.

Homemade Orange Soda

MAKES: about 2½ qt. | **HANDS-ON TIME:** 5 min. | **TOTAL TIME:** 5 min.

1   **(12-oz.) can frozen, pulp-free orange juice concentrate, thawed**
2   **(2-liter) bottles lemon-lime soft drink, chilled**
1   **to 2 oranges, thinly sliced**

1. Stir together orange juice concentrate and lemon-lime soft drink just before serving. Serve over ice in individual glasses with an orange slice. Stir occasionally to keep ingredients thoroughly mixed.

Fizzy Spiced Pomegranate Sipper

MAKES: 13 cups | **HANDS-ON TIME:** 10 min. | **TOTAL TIME:** 3 hr.

1   **(2½-inch) cinnamon stick**
5   **whole cloves**
5   **thin fresh ginger slices**
2   **(16-oz.) bottles refrigerated 100% pomegranate juice**
4   **cups white grape juice**
½   **cup pineapple juice**
1   **(1-liter) bottle ginger ale**

1. Cook cinnamon stick, cloves, and ginger in a Dutch oven over medium heat, stirring constantly, 2 to 3 minutes or until cinnamon is fragrant.
2. Gradually stir in juices. Bring to a boil over medium-high heat; reduce heat to medium-low, and simmer 15 minutes. Pour mixture through a wire-mesh strainer into a heatproof pitcher; discard solids.
3. Let stand 30 minutes. Cover and chill 2 hours. Store in refrigerator up to 2 days. Stir in ginger ale just before serving, and serve over ice.
Note: We tested with POM Wonderful 100% Pomegranate Juice and Welch's 100% White Grape Juice.

Customize Berry Splash by adding more sugar for a sweeter drink, ¼ cup at a time, until it's just the way you like it.

Aubie and members of the Auburn Dance Line get ready for Tiger Walk. Aubie holds seven National Mascot Championship wins and is the winningest mascot in collegiate history.

Sparkling Autumn Sipper

MAKES: about 7 cups | **HANDS-ON TIME:** 15 min. | **TOTAL TIME:** 2 hr., 15 min.

1	**Bartlett pear**
3	**small Pink Lady or Gala apples**
3	**fresh plums, cut into wedges**
½	**cup cane syrup**
2	**(4-inch) fresh rosemary sprigs**
1	**vanilla bean, split**
3½	**cups grape juice**
1	**(750-milliliter) bottle sparkling white grape juice, chilled**

Garnish: fresh rosemary sprigs

1. Cut pear lengthwise into ¼-inch slices, cutting from stem end through the bottom. Cut apples crosswise into ¼-inch slices.

2. Stir together pear, apples, plums, and next 3 ingredients in a 3-qt. glass container until fruit is coated. Gradually stir in grape juice. Cover and chill 2 to 24 hours.

3. Stir in sparkling white grape juice just before serving. Serve over ice.

Arnold Palmer

MAKES: 1 serving | **HANDS-ON TIME:** 5 min. | **TOTAL TIME:** 5 min.

Iced tea
Lemonade

1. Serve equal parts iced tea and lemonade over ice.

 Extra Point: Garnish with lavender. Its soft, floral flavor contrasts with the sharpness of the lemonade in this classic iced tea "mocktail."

Bloody Mary Punch

MAKES: 1½ qt. | **HANDS-ON TIME:** 10 min. | **TOTAL TIME:** 10 min.

1	**(46-oz.) container low-sodium vegetable juice, chilled**
1	**Tbsp. freshly ground pepper**
3	**Tbsp. fresh lime juice**
1	**Tbsp. hot sauce**
1	**Tbsp. Worcestershire sauce**
½	**tsp. Old Bay seasoning**

Celery sticks (optional)

1. Combine first 6 ingredients in a punch bowl or pitcher. Serve over ice with celery sticks, if desired.

Note: We tested with V8 Low Sodium 100% Vegetable Juice.

Double or triple the recipe for Bloody Mary Punch and offer assorted garnishes such as celery sticks, carrot sticks, pickled okra, and lemon and lime wedges.

Sparkling Autumn Sipper

Hurricane Punch

Hurricane Punch

MAKES: 17½ cups | **HANDS-ON TIME:** 5 min. | **TOTAL TIME:** 5 min.

1 (64-oz.) bottle red fruit punch
1 (12-oz.) can frozen limeade concentrate, thawed
1 (64-oz.) bottle orange juice
Garnishes: orange and lime slices, fresh mint

1. Stir together all ingredients. Serve over ice.

Raspberry-Ginger Ale Cocktail

MAKES: 8 cups | **HANDS-ON TIME:** 5 min. | **TOTAL TIME:** 5 min.

¾ cup fresh or frozen raspberries
3½ (12-oz.) bottles ginger ale, chilled
1 (12-oz.) can frozen raspberry lemonade concentrate, thawed
½ cup tonic water

1. Stir together all ingredients. Serve over ice.

Carolina Peach Punch

MAKES: about 7 cups | **HANDS-ON TIME:** 10 min. | **TOTAL TIME:** 8 hr., 10 min.

4 cups white grape juice
½ cup peach nectar
2 Tbsp. sugar
6 Tbsp. thawed frozen lemonade concentrate
1 lb. ripe peaches, peeled and sliced
1 (6-oz.) package fresh raspberries
2 cups club soda, chilled
Garnishes: peach slices, raspberries

1. Combine first 4 ingredients in a pitcher; stir until sugar is dissolved. Stir in peaches and raspberries. Cover and chill 8 hours.
2. Stir in chilled club soda just before serving.

Pour Hurricane Punch into plastic pop molds and freeze until firm for an extra-refreshing treat.

Fresh peaches and raspberries add pizzazz to this make-ahead Carolina Peach Punch.

Swamp®

Hot. Humid. Hostile.
The Swamp is a miserable place to play—unless you're a Gator®.
Then it's a little slice of heaven.

For years, Ben Hill Griffin Stadium—a.k.a. The Swamp—has been one of the most dreaded road trip destinations in college football. The odds of claiming a victory here are roughly equivalent to those of winning the lottery. Not impossible, just improbable.

The enclosed stadium sits in a sinkhole with the playing surface and first 32 rows of seats below ground level. There's little breeze. The Florida team bench sits in the shade, while opponents roast in the still-blazing autumn sun. Game-time temperatures at Florida Field regularly soar past the 100-degree mark.

Though opponents wilt under the punishing Florida heat, real Gators flourish. After tailgating for hours, some 90,000 screaming fans move into The Swamp for the main event. Their menacing Gator Chomp is a universal sign of disdain. By the end of the third quarter, when they stand, lock arms, and sway in unison, singing "We ARE the Boys of Old Florida," the victory celebration is usually well under way. "When you walk into The Swamp on game day, you can taste a victory," says one hungry Gator.

Still, this was never called The Swamp until the irascible Steve Spurrier came back to town. He quarterbacked at Florida, won a Heisman, and returned to coach in the '90s. It was he who said only Gators get out alive.

The theme music from the movie *Jaws* fills the stadium as the players come out of the tunnel and hit the field.

Gainesville, FL

FLORIDA

Lake Alice—an on-campus freshwater lake—is a haven for students and gators alike.

We don't know how Lake Alice got its name, but we do know it was called Jonah's Pond prior to the 1890s.

Florida is the only university in the nation with a gator as its mascot. A visit to the school reveals why this choice makes so much sense. There are alligators on campus—wild and untamed—roaming free at lovely Lake Alice.

Once part of the farm that became the university, this small freshwater lake sits at the heart of the rambling Gainesville campus and welcomes visitors daily. Oaks dripping with Spanish moss line the banks, and a boardwalk bridges the wetlands. The Baughman Center, a soaring cypress-and-glass chapel on the lake's southwestern shore, offers sanctuary for those seeking a private place to meditate. See the next page for other Gainesville greats.

Best Places to Spot Gators

A haven for wildlife of every description, the man-made lake is also home to herons, turtles, and a massive colony of Brazilian free-tail bats that emerge at night to eat their weight in insects. "Lots of people come here just to see the alligators," says **Baughman Center** manager and UF alum Lizz Nehls. "It's a peaceful bit of nature right in the middle of campus. You can get away from it all, but you don't have to go very far to do it."

Outdoor Adventures

For the recreation seekers, bikers can ride the 16-mile paved Gainesville-Hawthorne State Trail all the way to **Paynes Prairie Preserve State Park** in nearby Micanopy. A 50-foot observation tower gives a panoramic view of the 22,000-acre wetland prairie where alligators, bison, and wild horses roam free. Nothing could be more Florida than canoeing, kayaking, tubing, or diving in one of the state's natural springs. College students favor privately owned **Ginnie Springs,** north of Gainesville, but both **Poe Springs** and **Blue Spring** are family friendly.

Where the Locals Eat

There's no more congenial place than quirky, loveable **Satchel's Pizza.** Folk art, hubcaps, and found objects cover the walls, inside and out, and visitors can dine in the old VW van parked out front. A resident peacock roosts nearby.

For those looking for a party, the Midtown area just across from **Ben Hill Griffin Stadium** on University Avenue is the place to find it. "During the day, there are great places to grab lunch or dinner," Gator Mike Herchel explains. "Then at night, there are bars where you can party it up."

Once a professor's home, **The Swamp Restaurant** is a favorite sports bar for Gators, and locals swear by **Burrito Bros. Taco Co.** for homemade guacamole and affordable Mexican food. The **Copper Monkey,** a popular campus pub that serves steak burgers and gourmet sandwiches, is another good spot to grab a bite.

For more information: **Alachua County Visitors & Convention Bureau, 866/778-5002** or **352/374-5260.**

Baughman Center

The Swamp Restaurant

Florida Gators®
Menu

Ginger-Orange Gator Tail Sipper
(recipe below)

Gator Bait (Fresh Salsa and Chips) (page 77)

Cuban Black Bean Dip (page 86)

Poblano Fish Tacos (page 136)

Tequila-Lime-Coconut Macaroon Bars
(page 227)

Keep ingredients well chilled, and stir together this orange-infused spirit sparker once you arrive at your tailgating location.

Ginger-Orange Gator Tail Sipper

MAKES: about 1½ gal. | **HANDS-ON TIME:** 5 min. | **TOTAL TIME:** 5 min.

1   **(89-oz.) container orange juice**
1   **(2-liter) bottle ginger ale, chilled**
1   **(46-oz.) can pineapple juice, chilled**
Garnishes: orange slices, fresh mint sprigs

1. Stir together orange juice, ginger ale, and pineapple juice. Serve over ice.

SEC Team Spritzers

The winner? It's a toss-up. Raise a glass and make a toast. May the best team come out on top. (Oh, and by the way, if you choose to make these beverages, let's just say—more spirited—your secret's safe with us.)

Kentucky Colonel

Muddle 5 mint leaves, 3 lemon slices, 2 Tbsp. turbinado sugar, and 1 Tbsp. fresh lemon juice in a 10-oz. glass. Fill glass with crushed ice, and top with seltzer water or club soda. Gently stir. Garnish with a lemon slice.

LSU Purple Prowler

Muddle ¼ cup fresh blackberries, 2 Tbsp. turbinado sugar, and 1 Tbsp. fresh lime juice in a 10-oz. glass. Fill glass with crushed ice, and top with seltzer water or club soda. Gently stir. Garnish with fresh blackberries and a lime rind strip.

Alabama Yella Hamma

Muddle ¼ cup diced fresh pineapple, ¼ cup fresh orange juice, and 2 Tbsp. turbinado sugar in a 10-oz. glass. Fill glass with crushed ice, and top with seltzer water or club soda. Gently stir. Garnish with a maraschino cherry and pineapple chunks.

Texas A&M Howdy

Muddle 3 lime wedges and 2 Tbsp. turbinado sugar in a 10-oz. glass. Add ½ cup ginger beer. Fill glass with crushed ice, and top with seltzer water or club soda. Gently stir. Garnish with a lime rind strip.

Florida Flojito

Muddle 5 cucumber slices, 4 lime wedges, 2 Tbsp. turbinado sugar, and 1 Tbsp. fresh lime juice in a 10-oz. glass. Fill glass with crushed ice, and top with seltzer water or club soda. Gently stir. Garnish with a cucumber slice.

Mizzou Brew

Gently muddle 2 lemon slices, 2 Tbsp. simple syrup (see Extra Point, page 71), and ½ tsp. root beer extract in a 10-oz. glass. Fill glass with crushed ice, and top with seltzer water or club soda. Gently stir. Garnish with a fresh lemon slice.

Tennessee Smoky Sipper

Stir together ¼ cup grapefruit juice, 2 Tbsp. honey, and 1 Tbsp. fresh lime juice in a 10-oz. glass. Fill glass with crushed ice, and top with seltzer water or club soda. Gently stir. Garnish with fresh lime and grapefruit slices.

MS State Bulldog Bloody Mary

Muddle 2 lemon wedges, 1 tsp. refrigerated horseradish, ½ tsp. hot sauce, and ¼ tsp. freshly ground pepper in a 10-oz. glass. Add 1 (5.5-oz.) can spicy vegetable juice. Fill glass with crushed ice, and top with seltzer water or club soda. Gently stir. Garnish with celery leaves and pickled okra.

Arkansas Razorback Red

Muddle ½ cup fresh raspberries, ¼ cup fruit punch, and 2 Tbsp. turbinado sugar in a 10-oz. glass. Fill glass with crushed ice, and top with seltzer water or club soda. Gently stir. Garnish with a fresh orange slice.

Vanderbilt Commodore

Gently muddle 1 orange rind strip and 2 Tbsp. turbinado sugar in a 10-oz. glass. Stir in ¼ cup apple cider, 2 Tbsp. fresh orange juice, and a pinch of ground cinnamon. Fill glass with crushed ice, and top with seltzer water or club soda. Gently stir. Garnish with a cinnamon stick and an orange rind strip.

Ole Miss "Ole" Fashioned

Muddle 2 orange slices, 2 Tbsp. turbinado sugar, 2 Tbsp. fresh orange juice, and 3 dashes bitters in a 10-oz. glass. Fill glass with crushed ice, and top with seltzer water or club soda. Gently stir. Garnish with an orange rind strip and a maraschino cherry.

Auburn Blue & Orangeade

Muddle ¼ cup fresh blueberries, 2 Tbsp. turbinado sugar, 2 Tbsp. fresh orange juice, and 2 Tbsp. fresh lemon juice in a 10-oz. glass. Fill glass with crushed ice, and top with seltzer water or club soda. Gently stir. Garnish with an orange wedge.

South Carolina Foghorn Leghorn

Muddle ¼ cup fresh raspberries; 3 medium strawberries, quartered; 2 Tbsp. turbinado sugar; and 2 Tbsp. fresh orange juice in a 10-oz. glass. Fill glass with crushed ice, and top with seltzer water or club soda. Gently stir. Garnish with a fresh strawberry.

Georgia Peach

Muddle ½ fresh peach, peeled; 3 mint leaves; 2 Tbsp. turbinado sugar; and 2 Tbsp. fresh orange juice in a 10-oz. glass. Fill glass with crushed ice, and top with seltzer water or club soda. Gently stir. Garnish with peach wedges and fresh mint.

Extra Point: Make your own simple syrup by cooking equal parts sugar and water over medium-high heat until sugar dissolves. Chill until ready to use.

Mini Muffulettas, page 88

(4)

CRUNCH TIME

From chips and dippers to light bites and heavier hitters, these gotta-have pre- and post-game goodies are a true tailgater's dream.

Rocky Top Popcorn

MAKES: 2 to 3 servings | **HANDS-ON TIME:** 20 min. | **TOTAL TIME:** 20 min.

4	bacon slices	4	Tbsp. butter, melted
1	(1.3-oz.) bag popped microwave popcorn	2	tsp. buttermilk Ranch dressing mix
¼	cup grated Parmesan cheese	¼	tsp. freshly ground pepper

1. Cook bacon in a large skillet over medium-high heat 10 minutes or until crisp; remove bacon, and drain on paper towels. Coarsely chop bacon. Pour popped popcorn into a large bowl. Toss with bacon, Parmesan cheese, melted butter, and buttermilk Ranch dressing mix. Sprinkle with freshly ground pepper, and serve immediately.

Note: We tested with Orville Redenbacher's Natural Simply Salted 50% Less Fat Gourmet Popping Corn.

Microwave Snack Mix

MAKES: 13 cups | **HANDS-ON TIME:** 15 min. | **TOTAL TIME:** 45 min.

2	(1-oz.) envelopes Ranch dressing mix	3	cups crisp wheat cereal squares
½	cup vegetable oil	2	cups pretzel sticks
3	cups crisp oatmeal cereal squares		Wax paper
3	cups corn-and-rice cereal	1	cup dried cherries
		1	cup candy-coated chocolate pieces

1. Whisk together Ranch dressing mix and oil in a large microwave-safe glass bowl. Stir in oatmeal cereal squares and next 3 ingredients.

2. Microwave mixture at HIGH 2 minutes, and stir well. Microwave at HIGH 2 more minutes, and stir well. Spread mixture in a single layer on wax paper, and let cool 30 minutes. Add cherries and candy pieces. Store in an airtight container up to 5 days.

Note: We tested with Quaker Essentials Oatmeal Squares for crisp oatmeal cereal squares, Crispix for corn-and-rice cereal, and Wheat Chex for wheat cereal squares.

Make a substitution—use pretzel sticks if you can't find rye chips.

Easy Tailgate Snack Mix

MAKES: about 10 cups | **HANDS-ON TIME:** 10 min. | **TOTAL TIME:** 17 min.

½	Tbsp. butter	2	cups garlic rye chips
1	cup salted almonds	1	(8.5-oz.) package sesame sticks
1	(9.9-oz.) can wasabi peas		

1. Preheat oven to 350°. Melt butter in a 9-inch cake pan in oven. Add nuts, and toss to coat. Bake 7 minutes or until lightly toasted; remove from oven.

2. Toss together nuts, wasabi peas, garlic rye chips, and sesame sticks in a large bowl. Store in an airtight container up to 1 week.

Note: We tested with Hapi Snacks Wasabi Peas, Gardetto's Special Request Roasted Garlic Rye Chips, and Pepperidge Farm Baked Naturals Toasted Sesame Snack Sticks.

Rocky Top Popcorn

Beer-Batter Fried Pickles

Beer-Batter Fried Pickles

MAKES: 8 to 10 servings | **HANDS-ON TIME:** 20 min. | **TOTAL TIME:** 25 min., including sauce

2   **(16-oz.) jars dill pickle sandwich slices, drained**
1   **large egg**
1   **(12-oz.) can beer**
1   **Tbsp. baking powder**
1   **tsp. seasoned salt**
1½ **cups all-purpose flour**
Vegetable oil
Spicy Ranch Dipping Sauce

1. Pat pickles dry with paper towels.

2. Whisk together egg and next 3 ingredients in a large bowl; add 1½ cups flour, and whisk until smooth.

3. Pour oil to depth of 1½ inches into a large heavy skillet or Dutch oven; heat over medium-high heat to 375°.

4. Dip pickle slices into batter, allowing excess batter to drip off. Fry pickles, in batches, 3 to 4 minutes or until golden. Drain and pat dry on paper towels; serve immediately with Spicy Ranch Dipping Sauce.

Spicy Ranch Dipping Sauce

MAKES: about 1 cup | **HANDS-ON TIME:** 5 min. | **TOTAL TIME:** 5 min.

¾   **cup buttermilk**
½   **cup mayonnaise**
2   **Tbsp. minced green onions**
1   **garlic clove, minced**
1   **tsp. hot sauce**
½   **tsp. seasoned salt**

1. Whisk together all ingredients. Store in an airtight container in refrigerator up to 2 weeks.

Gator Bait (Fresh Salsa and Chips)

MAKES: about 4 cups | **HANDS-ON TIME:** 20 min. | **TOTAL TIME:** 20 min.

¼   **medium-size sweet onion, coarsely chopped**
1   **small garlic clove, quartered**
1   **jalapeño pepper, seeded and quartered**
¼   **cup loosely packed fresh cilantro leaves**
2   **lb. tomatoes**
1   **lime, halved**
1¼ **tsp. salt**
Tortilla chips

1. Pulse first 4 ingredients in a food processor until finely chopped.

2. Cut each tomato into 4 pieces. Cut core away from each piece; discard core. Add tomatoes to food processor in batches, and pulse each batch until well blended. Transfer to a large bowl. Squeeze juice from lime over salsa, and stir in salt. Serve with chips.

Tantalizing tomato deliciousness or Gator Bait. You decide.

FOR WHOM THE

Bell Tolls

"Freshmen used to have this job," a red-and-black-clad alum explains. "Now anybody can ring the bell. You jump as high as you can, grab onto the rope, and pull with all your might. The momentum lifts you waaaaay off the ground!"

As night blankets the University of Georgia, a deep, throaty bell rings through the darkening hours, bringing smiles to Bulldog fans all across Athens. Even if they didn't go to the game or check the score, the Chapel Bell tells them the Dawgs claimed another victory today.

The Chapel Bell sits on the North Campus Quad near Herty Field, the school's original gridiron, named for the chemistry professor who coached the first Georgia football team in 1892. Though the bell once roused sleepy students, it now caps a long, glorious game day at UGA.

Georgia football is as steeped in tradition as any program in the nation. Tailgaters are allowed to start setting up at 7 a.m. on game day, and soon breakfast perfumes the air. By the time lunch rolls around, a gigantic backyard barbecue is under way.

Because privet hedges surround the Sanford Stadium field, the Dawgs play "Between The Hedges." They don't wear uniforms—they wear silver britches. Uga, the team's English bulldog mascot, has graced the cover of *Sports Illustrated* and starred in a movie.

As for departing rivals, here's one little piece of advice: Ask not for whom the Chapel Bell tolls. It tolls for thee, y'all.

Since 1956, Uga, an English bulldog, has served as the mascot for the University of Georgia. His sideline presence is as iconic as the UGA fight song, "Glory, Glory."

Athens, GA

"The Arch is the symbol of the university and acts as the gateway into campus

The Arch was built in the late 1850s as part of an iron fence erected to secure the campus.

A graceful black iron arch with three narrow pillars sits at the edge of Georgia's picture-perfect North Campus, facing Broad Street and downtown Athens. Generations of UGA students have walked beneath this arch—or not, if they happen to be superstitious.

"The Arch is the symbol of the university, and it acts as the gateway into campus," says former UGA cheerleader Clif Sandlin. "For many years, students were forbidden to walk beneath the arch until they graduated. Now, most voluntarily forgo the privilege as a sign of respect."

Grown-Up College Town

The three pillars stand for wisdom, justice, and moderation, the ideals upon which the University of Georgia was built in 1785. City leaders bought land for the university, one of the country's oldest, and sold lots to help raise funds. By the time the first class graduated, a little village was beginning to take root. Today, the University of Georgia is a mighty educational force, and Athens is a grown-up college town with an irresistibly quirky, offbeat personality.

"The thing that is so great about Athens is that it has everything a big city has without the stress and the traffic," says Barbara Dooley, who moved here in 1963 when her husband, Vince, became head football coach. "The city has done a magnificent job of keeping its downtown alive. There's always something going on around here."

Fan Fare

Many in the Classic City start their day with a stack of hotcakes or biscuits and gravy at **The Mayflower**, an old-school diner just across from the Arch. **Weaver D's** slogan — "Automatic for the People"— became the title of a Grammy-nominated R.E.M. album, but this spot is famous in its own right for soul food served family-style. Locals beat a path to **Mama's Boy** for treats such as Georgia Peach French Toast and a Grilled Pimiento Cheese Burger.

New South Flavors

Once a popular music venue, **Last Resort Grill** now serves the flavors of the New South, including pork belly, pecan-crusted blue trout, and mouthwatering desserts. Homemade Southern sides take center stage

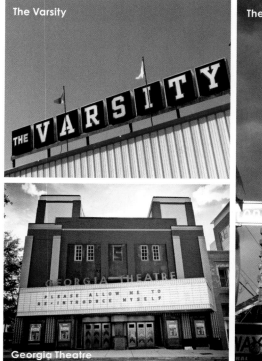

The Varsity

Georgia Theatre

PLEASE ALLOW ME TO RE/INTRODUCE MYSELF

The Grit

at **The Grit**, a vegetarian hot spot for hungry rockers. UGA and Georgia Tech don't agree on much—except **The Varsity**. The legendary drive-in with locations in Athens, metro Atlanta, and Dawsonville serves chili dogs, onion rings, and frosted orange milk shakes.

Top Chef judge Hugh Acheson began his culinary rise in the Classic City. With its ever-changing menu and New South flavors, his **Five & Ten** on Lumpkin Street is a staple for fine dining. Acheson's downtown restaurant, **The National,** has creative Mediterranean flavors and an alluring cocktail list.

Hall of Fame

Sports fans can relive UGA's moments of glory and get a close-up view of Hershel Walker's Heisman Trophy at **Butts-Mehre Heritage Hall** on campus. Not only does it house athletic offices and training facilities, it's also home to the Georgia Bulldog Hall of Fame. Be sure to note the

building's elevator buttons—one says Hunker Up, the other Hunker Down, a reference to a call by longtime radio play-by-play announcer Larry Munson.

World-Class Music Scene

When the lights go down in Athens, the volume goes up on a first-rate music scene. Some of the country's most celebrated musicians not only play here, they live here too. Rock, country, alternative—no matter what type you like, you'll find it. Consult the local *Flagpole* magazine for a complete list of music venues. Popular venues include the **40 Watt Club**, the **Georgia Theatre**, and the **Melting Point,** as well as the small, friendly **Caledonia Lounge** and the **Flicker Theatre & Bar.**

For more information: **Athens Convention & Visitors Bureau, 706/357-4430.**

Georgia Bulldogs® Menu

Hot Spiced Boiled Peanuts
(recipe below)

Baked Vidalia Onion Dip (page 93)

Sweet Heat Hot Dogs (page 150)

Root Beer Baked Beans
(page 185)

Peach Melba Shortbread Bars
(page 227)

Make up to two days before the game. Get in the spirit, and serve in cups in your team colors.

Hot Spiced Boiled Peanuts

MAKES: about 4 cups | **HANDS-ON TIME:** 10 min. | **TOTAL TIME:** 5 hr., 25 min.

2	lb. raw peanuts in the shell
¾	cup hot sauce
⅓	cup salt
1	(3-inch) piece fresh ginger, sliced
1	Tbsp. black peppercorns
2	tsp. coriander seeds
2	bay leaves

1. Bring all ingredients and 1 gal. water to a boil in a stockpot over high heat. Cover, reduce heat to medium-low, and cook, stirring occasionally, 4 hours or until peanuts are tender. Add water as needed to keep peanuts covered.

2. Remove from heat; let stand, covered, 1 hour.

Note: We tested with Texas Pete Original Hot Sauce.

This all-American snack pairs perfectly with your favorite burger or barbecue recipe. Don't be afraid to sprinkle with different seasoning blends instead of salt for a new twist.

Make it a mini slider! Get a little saucy, and stuff rectangular party-style or dinner rolls with meatballs or sausage bites.

From-Scratch Oven Fries

MAKES: 4 servings | **HANDS-ON TIME:** 20 min. | **TOTAL TIME:** 1 hr.

1½	lb. medium-size baking potatoes, peeled and cut into ½-inch-thick strips	1	Tbsp. vegetable oil
		½	tsp. kosher or table salt
			Ketchup (optional)

1. Preheat oven to 450°. Rinse potatoes in cold water. Drain and pat dry. Toss together potatoes, oil, and salt in a large bowl.

2. Place a lightly greased wire rack in a jelly-roll pan. Arrange potatoes in a single layer on a wire rack.

3. Bake at 450° for 40 to 45 minutes or until browned. Serve immediately with ketchup, if desired.

Buffalo Oven Fries: Omit salt. Toss 2 tsp. mesquite seasoning, 1 tsp. hot sauce, ½ tsp. celery salt, and ½ tsp. garlic powder with potatoes and vegetable oil; bake as directed. Serve with blue cheese dressing and bottled hot wing sauce, if desired.

Italian-Parmesan Oven Fries: Toss 2 tsp. freshly ground Italian seasoning with potato mixture, and bake as directed. Sprinkle warm fries with 2 Tbsp. grated Parmesan cheese. Serve with warm marinara sauce, if desired.
Note: We tested with McCormick Italian Herb Seasoning Grinder.

Spicy Cheese Oven Fries: Toss a pinch of ground red pepper with potato mixture, and bake as directed. Sprinkle with ⅓ cup (1½ oz.) shredded reduced-fat pepper Jack cheese. Bake 1 more minute or until cheese is melted. Serve with ketchup, if desired.

Chipotle-Barbecue Meatballs

MAKES: 12 to 14 appetizer servings | **HANDS-ON TIME:** 10 min. | **TOTAL TIME:** 1 hr., 10 min.

1	(28-oz.) bottle barbecue sauce	1	Tbsp. adobo sauce from can
1	(18-oz.) jar cherry preserves	1	(32-oz.) package frozen meatballs
3	canned chipotle peppers in adobo sauce		

1. Whisk together first 4 ingredients and 1½ cups water in a Dutch oven. Bring to a boil over medium-high heat. Add meatballs; return to a boil. Reduce heat to medium, and simmer, stirring occasionally, 40 to 45 minutes. (Sauce will thicken.) Keep warm in a slow cooker on WARM or LOW, if desired.
Note: We tested with Rosina Italian Style Meatballs.

Chipotle-Barbecue Sausage Bites: Substitute 2 (16-oz.) packages cocktail-size smoked sausages for meatballs. Proceed with recipe as directed, decreasing water to ½ cup and simmering mixture 15 minutes. Hands-on Time: 10 min., Total Time: 30 min.

Fried Chicken Bites

MAKES: 4 to 6 servings | **HANDS-ON TIME:** 50 min. | **TOTAL TIME:** 50 min., plus 24 hr. to marinate

1½	tsp. to 1 Tbsp. ground red pepper	½	tsp. paprika
1½	tsp. ground chipotle chile pepper	2	lb. skinned and boned chicken breasts
1½	tsp. garlic powder	2	cups buttermilk
1½	tsp. dried crushed red pepper	3	bread slices, toasted
1½	tsp. ground black pepper	1	cup all-purpose flour
¾	tsp. salt		Peanut oil
			Blue cheese dressing or honey mustard dressing

1. Combine first 7 ingredients in a small bowl; reserve half of spice mixture. Cut chicken into 1-inch pieces. Place chicken in a medium bowl, and toss with remaining spice mixture until coated. Stir in buttermilk; cover and chill 24 hours.

2. Tear bread into pieces, and place in a food processor with reserved spice mixture. Process until mixture resembles cornmeal. Stir in flour. Remove chicken pieces from buttermilk, discarding buttermilk. Dredge chicken in breadcrumb mixture.

3. Pour oil to depth of 2 inches into a Dutch oven; heat to 350°. Fry chicken, in batches, 6 to 7 minutes on each side or until golden brown and done. Drain on a wire rack over paper towels. Sprinkle with salt to taste. Serve warm or cold with blue cheese dressing or honey mustard dressing.

Extra Point: Stuff into mini tea biscuits for a breakfast the whole family will love. (Perfect on Sundays when you crave those chicken babies the most.)

Who doesn't love picnic-perfect cold fried chicken? Fry these the night before, and this snack becomes portable. It's sure to "Tide" over the hungriest football fanatics throughout the entire game.

Guacamole

MAKES: 3½ cups | **HANDS-ON TIME:** 10 min. | **TOTAL TIME:** 40 min.

5	ripe avocados	1	garlic clove, pressed
2	Tbsp. finely chopped red onion	¾	tsp. salt
2	Tbsp. fresh lime juice		Tortilla chips
½	medium-size jalapeño pepper, seeded and chopped		

1. Cut avocados in half. Scoop pulp into a bowl, and mash with a potato masher or fork until slightly chunky. Stir in chopped red onion and next 4 ingredients. Cover with plastic wrap, placing plastic wrap directly on surface of guacamole, and let stand at room temperature 30 minutes. Serve guacamole with tortilla chips.

Cilantro Guacamole: Prepare recipe as directed, stirring in 3 Tbsp. chopped fresh cilantro and an additional 1 Tbsp. fresh lime juice with onion.

Get in the game with this classic guacamole recipe. Keep guacamole from changing color by placing a layer of plastic wrap directly on the surface of the mixture while it stands for the flavors to meld.

Muffuletta Dip

MAKES: about 4 cups | **HANDS-ON TIME:** 20 min. | **TOTAL TIME:** 1 hr., 20 min.

1	cup Italian olive salad, drained	4	oz. provolone cheese, diced
1	cup diced salami (about 4 oz.)	1	celery rib, finely chopped
¼	cup grated Parmesan cheese	½	red bell pepper, chopped
¼	cup chopped pepperoncini salad peppers	1	Tbsp. olive oil
1	(2¼-oz.) can sliced black olives, drained	¼	cup chopped fresh parsley
			French bread crostini

1. Stir together first 9 ingredients. Cover and chill 1 to 24 hours before serving. Stir in parsley just before serving. Serve with French bread crostini. Store leftovers in refrigerator up to 5 days.

Note: We tested with Boscoli Italian Olive Salad.

Texas A&M Caviar

MAKES: 6 cups | **HANDS-ON TIME:** 10 min. | **TOTAL TIME:** 10 min.

2	(15.5-oz.) cans black-eyed peas with jalapeño peppers, drained and rinsed	1	small green bell pepper, diced
		½	red onion, diced
		¾	cup zesty Italian dressing
1	(10-oz.) can diced tomatoes and green chiles	1	Tbsp. fresh lime juice
		¼	tsp. salt
2	avocados, diced		Corn chips

1. Stir together first 8 ingredients. Cover and chill, if desired. Serve with corn chips.

Cuban Black Bean Dip

MAKES: about 2 cups | **HANDS-ON TIME:** 15 min. | **TOTAL TIME:** 3 hr., 10 min.

1	(6-oz.) package Cuban-style black bean soup mix	2	Tbsp. Mexican crema or regular sour cream
1	Tbsp. olive oil		Fresh vegetable slices
2	Tbsp. fresh lime juice		Garnishes: diced tomatoes, thinly sliced green onions
½	tsp. ground cumin		
¼	tsp. ground chipotle chile powder		

1. Bring soup mix, olive oil, and 2½ cups water to a boil in a medium saucepan over high heat, stirring occasionally. Cover, reduce heat to low, and simmer, stirring occasionally, 25 minutes. Uncover and cook 5 to 7 minutes or until thick and beans are tender. Let cool 30 minutes.

2. Process soup mixture, lime juice, cumin, and chile powder in a food processor 20 seconds or until smooth. Spoon mixture into a serving bowl. Cover and chill 2 hours before serving. Store in refrigerator in an airtight container up to 2 days. Spread center of dip with Mexican crema. Serve with fresh vegetable slices.

Note: We tested with Nueva Cocina Cuban Style Black Bean Soup Mix and Olé Crema Mexicana.

Muffuletta Dip

Mini Muffulettas

MAKES: 12 appetizer servings | **HANDS-ON TIME:** 25 min. | **TOTAL TIME:** 25 min.

2	(16-oz.) jars mixed pickled vegetables	12	small dinner rolls, cut in half
¾	cup pimiento-stuffed Spanish olives, chopped	6	Swiss cheese slices, cut in half
2	Tbsp. bottled olive oil-and-vinegar dressing	12	thin deli ham slices
		12	Genoa salami slices
		6	provolone cheese slices, cut in half

1. Pulse pickled vegetables in a food processor 8 to 10 times or until finely chopped. Stir in olives and dressing.

2. Spread 1 heaping tablespoonful pickled vegetable mixture over cut side of each roll bottom. Top each with 1 Swiss cheese slice half, 1 ham slice, 1 salami slice, 1 provolone cheese slice half, and roll tops. Serve immediately, or cover with plastic wrap, and chill until ready to serve.

Note: We tested with Mezzetta Italian Mix Giardiniera pickled vegetables and Newman's Own Olive Oil & Vinegar dressing.

Bacon-Onion Dip

MAKES: 1¾ cups | **HANDS-ON TIME:** 10 min. | **TOTAL TIME:** 10 min.

1	(8-oz.) container sour cream	1	Tbsp. refrigerated horseradish
½	cup cooked and crumbled bacon	2	tsp. fresh lemon juice
2	Tbsp. green onions, sliced	¼	tsp. pepper
3	Tbsp. buttermilk	½	tsp. salt
			Potato chips

1. Stir together first 8 ingredients. Cover and chill until ready to serve. Serve with chips.

If skinny dipping isn't your thing, take the plunge with crackers and potato chips.

Herbed Dip with Baby Vegetables

MAKES: 8 to 10 appetizer servings | **HANDS-ON TIME:** 15 min. | **TOTAL TIME:** 4 hr., 15 min.

1	cup mayonnaise	1	tsp. Beau Monde seasoning
½	cup sour cream	1	tsp. hot sauce
2	Tbsp. chopped fresh parsley	½	tsp. salt
1	Tbsp. finely chopped sweet onion	1	lb. thin fresh asparagus
1	Tbsp. chopped fresh dill	½	lb. haricots verts (tiny green beans), trimmed

1. Stir together first 8 ingredients in a small bowl until well blended. Cover and chill 4 to 24 hours.

2. Meanwhile, snap off and discard tough ends of asparagus. Cut asparagus into 6-inch pieces, reserving any remaining end portions for another use. Cook asparagus in boiling water to cover in a large saucepan 1 to 2 minutes or until crisp-tender; drain. Plunge into ice water to stop the cooking process; drain. Repeat procedure with haricots verts. Place vegetables in zip-top plastic bags; seal and chill until ready to serve. Serve mayonnaise mixture with chilled vegetables.

Mini Muffulettas

Layered Spicy Black Bean Dip

Layered Spicy Black Bean Dip

MAKES: 8 servings | HANDS-ON TIME: 10 min. | TOTAL TIME: 10 min.

1   (8-oz.) package cream cheese, softened
1   (16-oz.) jar spicy black bean dip
½   (8-oz.) package shredded Mexican four-cheese blend
Toppings: sliced green onions, chopped tomatoes, sliced black olives
Assorted tortilla and corn chips

1. Layer cream cheese, dip, and cheese in a 1-qt. serving dish. Add desired toppings, and serve with chips.
Note: We tested with Desert Pepper Trading Company Spicy Black Bean Dip.

Blue Cheese Ranch Dip

MAKES: 2½ cups | HANDS-ON TIME: 5 min. | TOTAL TIME: 5 min.

1   (16-oz.) container sour cream
1   (4-oz.) package blue cheese crumbles
1   (1-oz.) package Ranch dip mix
2   Tbsp. chopped fresh chives
Carrot and celery sticks, sturdy potato chips, and hot wings

1. Stir together first 4 ingredients. Serve with carrot and celery sticks, sturdy potato chips, and hot wings.

 Extra Point: Tackle bland sandwiches head-on, and use as a bread spread.

Loaded Baked Potato Dip

MAKES: about 4 cups | HANDS-ON TIME: 20 min. | TOTAL TIME: 1 hr., 30 min.

1   (2.1-oz.) package fully cooked bacon slices
1   (16-oz.) container sour cream
2   cups (8 oz.) freshly shredded sharp Cheddar cheese
⅓   cup sliced fresh chives
2   tsp. hot sauce
Warm waffle fries
Garnishes: cooked, crumbled bacon; sliced fresh chives; freshly cracked pepper

1. Microwave bacon according to package directions until crisp; drain on paper towels. Cool 10 minutes; crumble. Stir together bacon and next 4 ingredients. Cover and chill 1 to 24 hours before serving. Serve with crispy, warm waffle fries.
Note: We tested with Oscar Mayer Fully Cooked Bacon.

Make up to two days ahead, and layer the dip in a plastic container with a lid for easy traveling. Toss in an icy cooler, and grab the chips before hitting the road.

Make this crowd-pleaser up to two days ahead of time. We baked frozen waffle fries extra-crispy for our dippers.

Warm Turnip Green Dip

MAKES: 4 cups | **HANDS-ON TIME:** 25 min. | **TOTAL TIME:** 30 min.

5	bacon slices, chopped	1	(8-oz.) container sour cream
½	medium-size sweet onion, chopped	½	tsp. dried crushed red pepper
2	garlic cloves, chopped	¼	tsp. salt
¼	cup dry white wine	¾	cup freshly grated Parmesan cheese
1	(16-oz.) package frozen chopped turnip greens, thawed		Assorted crackers, flatbread, and gourmet wafers
12	oz. cream cheese, cut into pieces		

1. Preheat broiler with oven rack 6 inches from heat. Cook bacon in a Dutch oven over medium-high heat 5 to 6 minutes or until crisp; remove bacon, and drain on paper towels, reserving 1 Tbsp. drippings in Dutch oven.

2. Sauté onion and garlic in hot drippings 3 to 4 minutes. Add wine, and cook 1 to 2 minutes, stirring to loosen particles from bottom of Dutch oven. Stir in turnip greens, next 4 ingredients, and ½ cup Parmesan cheese. Cook, stirring often, 6 to 8 minutes or until cream cheese is melted and mixture is thoroughly heated. Transfer to a lightly greased 1½-qt. baking dish. (Make certain that you use a broiler-safe baking dish.) Sprinkle with remaining ¼ cup Parmesan cheese.

3. Broil 4 to 5 minutes or until cheese is lightly browned. Sprinkle with bacon. Serve with assorted crackers, flatbread, and wafers.

Warm Spinach-Artichoke Dip: Substitute 2 (10-oz.) packages frozen spinach, thawed and drained, and 1 (14-oz.) can quartered artichoke hearts, drained and coarsely chopped, for turnip greens. Proceed with recipe as directed.

Spicy Queso Dip

MAKES: about 3 cups | **HANDS-ON TIME:** 20 min. | **TOTAL TIME:** 20 min.

1	small onion, diced	1	(10-oz.) can diced tomatoes and green chiles
1	Tbsp. oil	2	Tbsp. chopped fresh cilantro
1	garlic clove, minced		Tortilla chips
1	(16-oz.) package pepper Jack pasteurized prepared cheese product, cubed		

1. Cook onion in hot oil in a large nonstick skillet over medium-high heat 8 minutes or until tender. Add garlic, and cook 1 minute. Remove from heat.

2. Combine cheese, tomatoes, and onion mixture in a large microwave-safe glass bowl. Microwave at HIGH 5 minutes, stirring every 2½ minutes. Stir in cilantro. Serve with tortilla chips.

Note: We tested with Velveeta Pepper Jack.

Extra Point: For a milder dip, prepare with regular pasteurized prepared cheese product. Spoon leftovers over baked potatoes or steamed broccoli.

With only six ingredients, this irresistible restaurant-style dip will be in high demand for all of your game-day gatherings and can be kept warm in a slow cooker.

Sausage, Bean, and Spinach Dip

MAKES: about 6 cups | **HANDS-ON TIME:** 20 min. | **TOTAL TIME:** 40 min.

1	sweet onion, diced	1	(6-oz.) package fresh baby
1	red bell pepper, diced		spinach, coarsely chopped
1	(1-lb.) package hot ground pork	¼	tsp. salt
	sausage	1	(15-oz.) can pinto beans,
2	garlic cloves, minced		drained and rinsed
1	tsp. chopped fresh thyme	½	cup (2 oz.) shredded
½	cup dry white wine		Parmesan cheese
1	(8-oz.) package cream cheese,		Corn chip scoops, red bell
	softened		pepper strips, pretzel rods

1. Preheat oven to 375°. Cook first 3 ingredients in a large skillet over medium-high heat, stirring often, 8 to 10 minutes or until meat crumbles and is no longer pink. Drain. Stir in garlic and thyme; cook 1 minute. Stir in wine; cook 2 minutes or until liquid has almost completely evaporated.

2. Add cream cheese, and cook, stirring constantly, 2 minutes or until cream cheese is melted. Stir in spinach and salt, and cook, stirring constantly, 2 minutes or until spinach is wilted. Gently stir in beans. Pour mixture into a 2-qt. baking dish; sprinkle with Parmesan cheese.

3. Bake at 375° for 18 to 20 minutes or until golden brown. Serve with corn chip scoops, bell pepper strips, and pretzel rods.

Pico de Gallo

MAKES: 6 cups | **HANDS-ON TIME:** 20 min. | **TOTAL TIME:** 1 hr., 20 min.

1	pt. grape tomatoes, chopped	1	garlic clove, pressed
1	green bell pepper, chopped	¾	tsp. salt
1	red bell pepper, chopped	½	tsp. ground cumin
1	avocado, peeled and chopped	½	tsp. lime zest
½	medium-size red onion, chopped	¼	cup fresh lime juice
½	cup chopped fresh cilantro		Tortilla or corn chips

1. Stir together first 11 ingredients; cover and chill 1 hour. Serve with tortilla or corn chips.

College students on College Avenue in June 1944. This route leads to the University of Georgia.

Baked Vidalia Onion Dip

MAKES: 6 cups | **HANDS-ON TIME:** 20 min. | **TOTAL TIME:** 55 min.

2	Tbsp. butter	1	(8-oz.) can sliced water
3	large Vidalia onions, coarsely		chestnuts, drained and chopped
	chopped	¼	cup dry white wine
2	cups (8 oz.) shredded Swiss	1	garlic clove, minced
	cheese	½	tsp. hot sauce
2	cups mayonnaise		Tortilla chips

1. Preheat oven to 375°. Melt butter in a large skillet over medium-high heat; add onion, and sauté 10 minutes or until tender.

2. Stir together shredded Swiss cheese and next 5 ingredients; stir in onion, blending well. Spoon mixture into a lightly greased 2-qt. baking dish.

3. Bake at 375° for 25 minutes, and let stand 10 minutes. Serve with tortilla chips.

HEAR THE

Trumpet's Call

A lone trumpeter tips his head back and sets the instrument to his lips. Then, with all his might, he sounds the familiar Call to Post. But he's not at a racetrack—he's starting the charge at Commonwealth Stadium.

"Whether you're at the racetrack or a football game, you know something special is about to happen when you hear that trumpet blow," says a Big Blue fan.

Lexington sits in the heart of bluegrass country, and the bugle call during the pregame show is a nod to the sport of kings. All eyes are on Kentucky for two minutes in May during the much-ballyhooed Derby, but equestrian pursuits are a way of life here year-round. In October, many football fans take in the fall races at nearby Keeneland before heading to the stadium.

No matter the sport, the quest for excellence is universal at UK. Even the tailgates feature a few only-in-the-bluegrass treats. Pots of Kentucky Burgoo, a meaty stew loaded with vegetables that dates back to pre-Civil War days, simmer away while flasks of fine bourbon are surreptitiously passed among friends.

By the time the Call to Post is sounded, Kentucky fans have gravitated to the stadium to cheer on the Wildcats. "Win or lose, we bleed blue here," boasts one UK follower. "We love our 'Cats!"

Memorial Hall is in central campus and was built in 1929 as a memorial to those who died in World War I. Today, it's used for lectures and performances.

Lexington, KY

Lexington sits amid the rolling hills of central Kentucky in the heart of horse country.

Kentucky Thoroughbred horses are the stars of Lexington. In 2010, the Kentucky Horse Park hosted the World Equestrian Games, the first time the games had been outside of Europe.

It's hard to imagine a prettier setting for a city—or a university. Lexington sits amid the rolling hills of central Kentucky in the heart of horse country, surrounded by picturesque farms and bluegrass meadows.

"It's not a small town, but it's not a large city either," says Kentucky Quarterback Club president Jim Wade. "Lexington has just about anything you could ever want or need."

That list includes a top-notch university. Like many schools, the University of Kentucky has grown in recent years, and the campus now has three main parts. Yet the heart and soul of the university remains Central Campus, home to the main entrance and beautiful Memorial Hall. "To me, this is where campus is and always will be," Jim says. "The white steeple of Memorial Hall is the symbol of UK."

The Land of Football and Horses

"Autumn is the perfect time to visit too," Jim says. As one of the northern-most schools in the Southeastern Conference, autumn comes first to the Bluegrass State. Crisp days mean two things in this part of Kentucky—football and horses.

"Find the horses, and you'll have a good time," UK alum Jennifer Allen confirms, and the **Kentucky Horse Park** is a great place to start.

One of the most beautiful racetracks in the country, **Keeneland** is the crown jewel of Lexington's equine industry. Visitors can explore beautiful paddocks and ivy-covered viewing stands or eat breakfast at the track kitchen any day of the year. Many UK fans begin their days at Keeneland before heading to Commonwealth Stadium for a football game.

At **Three Chimneys** in nearby Midway, visitors learn that Derby winner Big Brown favors butterscotch candy, while Point Given is partial to peppermint. "We're lucky enough to have the celebrity horses here," says communications director Jen Roytz.

Southern Comforts

In a town this size, it's possible to find just about anything you want to eat, but there are a few standard bearers. Open 24/7, **Tolly-Ho** is the ultimate college dive, best known for its burgers and all-day breakfast. **Joe Bologna's** has been a church, a synagogue, and now a pizza joint. Students rave about the pies, but the hot-from-the-oven breadsticks swimming in garlic butter are divine. A traditional meat 'n' three, **Ramsey's Diner** also serves a terrific Kentucky Hot Brown.

Keeneland

Many revelers flock to **Limestone Street,** or "the Party on Lime" as students call it. The street takes on a party atmosphere after a game and on weekends. Simply follow the crowd.

Locals rave about the family-owned **Merrick Inn,** a restaurant that occupies the manor house of a former horse farm and serves the flavors of the South. Specialties include fried chicken and pecan-crusted pork tenderloin. Then there's the Southern Comfort, a fried chicken breast with country ham and redeye gravy served with a spiced peach.

Uptown Dining Downtown

Downtown Lexington claims some of the region's best fine-dining establishments. Renaissance man Jonathan Lundy grew up on a horse farm, trained with chef Emeril Lagasse in New Orleans, and finally came home to open his own restaurant. The ultimate in fine dining, **Jonathan at Gratz Park** offers a new twist on traditional Kentucky dishes. Boiled peanuts, mint julep jelly, pork jowl cracklins, and bourbon are sprinkled throughout his menu.

Dudley's on Short, located in the beautiful Northern Bank Building downtown, is a local favorite for pumpkin ravioli at lunch and dinner. The blackboard specials at **Table Three Ten** are dictated by what's available from local farmers, and the 20-seat oak bar offers a great place to relax with a cheese plate and glass of fine wine.

For more information: **Lexington Convention & Visitors Bureau, 800/845-3959** or **859/233-7299.**

Three Chimneys

Kentucky Wildcats® Menu

Baked Bean Crostini
(recipe below)

Flank Steak Sandwiches with
"Go Big Blue®" Cheese (page 148)

Grilled Okra and Tomatoes (page 189)

Hot Bacon Potato Salad with
Green Beans (page 191)

Bourbon Balls (page 210)

Crunchy Pecan Pie Bites (page 212)

Try the baked beans alone or as a delicious side dish to any grilled meal. Simply sprinkle with cooked and crumbled bacon before serving.

Baked Bean Crostini

MAKES: 8 to 10 appetizer servings | **HANDS-ON TIME:** 30 min. | **TOTAL TIME:** 30 min.

1	(8.5-oz.) French bread baguette
	Vegetable cooking spray
5	thick hickory-smoked bacon slices
½	cup diced sweet onion
1	(28-oz.) can baked beans
3	Tbsp. apple cider vinegar
1	Tbsp. grated fresh ginger
1	Tbsp. yellow mustard
2	tsp. diced pickled jalapeño peppers
¼	tsp. salt

Toppings: chopped fresh rosemary, queso fresco (fresh Mexican cheese), spicy barbecue sauce, pickled jalapeño pepper slices, hot sauce

1. Preheat grill to 400° to 450° (high) heat. Cut bread into 40 (¼-inch-thick) slices, discarding ends. Coat 1 side of each bread slice with cooking spray. Grill bread slices, without grill lid, 1 to 2 minutes on each side.

2. Cook bacon in a large skillet over medium-high heat 8 to 10 minutes or until crisp; remove bacon, and drain on paper towels, reserving 2 Tbsp. drippings in skillet. Crumble bacon.

3. Sauté onion in hot drippings 5 minutes or until tender. Stir in beans and next 5 ingredients; cook over medium heat, stirring occasionally, 5 minutes or until thoroughly heated and slightly thickened. Spoon bean mixture onto grilled bread slices. Sprinkle with crumbled bacon. Serve with desired toppings.

Note: We tested with Bush's Best Country Style Baked Beans.

10 Ways to Get Your Game On with "The Pâté of the South"

1. Stuff into large Spanish olives for a no-cook popper.

2. Serve with sliced, tart Granny Smith apples.

3. Make the ultimate grilled cheese sandwich...add cooked bacon slices if you dare!

4. Spoon onto a grilled hot dog in a bun. Top with chili and onions.

5. Spoon onto hot fried green tomatoes for a crowd-pleasing appetizer.

6. Dollop on saltine crackers, and top with a dash of Asian Sriracha hot chili sauce and sweet-hot pickle chips.

7. Spread on toasted baguette slices, and top with a dollop of strawberry jam and sliced green onions.

8. Stuff into a seeded jalapeño pepper, wrap with bacon, and smoke slowly on a grill over 300° to 350° (medium) heat.

9. Smear on a graham cracker or gingersnap for a little sweet and savory treat.

10. Enjoy a post-game sami. Spread on white bread, and pack in your cooler to munch on after the game.

Southern-Style Pimiento Cheese

MAKES: about 3½ cups | **HANDS-ON TIME:** 15 min. | **TOTAL TIME:** 15 min.

- **4 cups (16 oz.) shredded sharp Cheddar cheese**
- **1 (4-oz.) jar diced pimientos, drained**
- **1 (3-oz.) package cream cheese, softened**
- **¾ cup mayonnaise**
- **1 tsp. paprika**
- **¼ tsp. salt**

1. Stir together all ingredients in a large bowl until blended.

Jalapeño-Pecan Pimiento Cheese: Stir in ⅓ cup chopped toasted pecans and ⅓ cup chopped jarred sweet-hot pickled jalapeño pepper slices.
Note: We tested with The Original Texas Sweet & Hot jalapeños.

Smoky Pimiento Cheese: Reduce sharp Cheddar cheese to 2 cups. Add 2 cups (8 oz.) shredded smoked Cheddar cheese. Proceed with recipe as directed.

Super-Quick Chili,
page 120

(5)

BEST BOWLS

Get bowled over by the best soups, chilis, and stews the Southeastern Conference has to offer. For a cool, crisp day in the fall, there's nothing more fitting—or filling.

Use your favorite frozen greens in this minestrone, or substitute a bag of thoroughly washed fresh spinach.

Southern Tortellini Minestrone

MAKES: 8 to 10 servings | **HANDS-ON TIME:** 20 min. | **TOTAL TIME:** 1 hr.

1	medium onion, chopped	1	(16-oz.) package chopped frozen collard greens
1	Tbsp. olive oil		
3	garlic cloves, chopped	3	Tbsp. chopped fresh parsley
2	(32-oz.) containers chicken broth	1	Tbsp. chopped fresh rosemary
¾	cup dry white wine	½	tsp. dried crushed red pepper
2	(14.5-oz.) cans Italian-style diced tomatoes	1	(16-oz.) package frozen cheese tortellini
1	(16-oz.) package frozen green beans		

1. Sauté onion in hot oil in a large Dutch oven over medium heat 8 minutes or until onion is tender. Add garlic, and cook 1 minute. Stir in chicken broth, white wine, and tomatoes; bring to a boil over medium-high heat. Add green beans, collard greens, and next 3 ingredients. Reduce heat to medium, and simmer, stirring occasionally, 15 minutes. Add pasta, and cook 10 to 12 minutes or until pasta is done.

Cheddar Cheese Soup

MAKES: 8 cups | **HANDS-ON TIME:** 35 min. | **TOTAL TIME:** 35 min.

¼	cup butter	⅓	cup all-purpose flour
½	cup finely chopped carrots	1	extra-large chicken bouillon cube
½	cup finely chopped celery		
1	small onion, finely chopped	2	cups milk
½	small green bell pepper, finely chopped	1	(8-oz.) block sharp Cheddar cheese, shredded
2	garlic cloves, minced	¼	tsp. ground red pepper

1. Melt butter in a 3-qt. saucepan over medium-high heat; add carrots and next 4 ingredients, and sauté 5 to 7 minutes or until tender. Sprinkle flour over vegetable mixture, and stir until coated. Stir in bouillon cube, milk, and 3 cups water; cook, stirring occasionally, 10 to 11 minutes or until mixture is slightly thickened and bubbly.

2. Add shredded cheese and red pepper, stirring until well blended. Serve immediately.

Southern Tortellini Minestrone

Taco Soup

Taco Soup

MAKES: 14 cups | **HANDS-ON TIME:** 10 min. | **TOTAL TIME:** 55 min.

- 1   lb. ground beef
- 2   (16-oz.) cans pinto beans, drained and rinsed
- 1   (16-oz.) package frozen cut green beans
- 1   (15-oz.) can ranch beans, undrained
- 1   (14.5-oz.) can Mexican-style stewed tomatoes
- 1   (14.5-oz.) can petite diced tomatoes, undrained
- 1   (12-oz.) package frozen whole kernel corn
- 1   (12-oz.) bottle beer*
- 1   (1-oz.) envelope taco seasoning mix
- 1   (1-oz.) envelope Ranch dressing mix

Toppings: corn chips, shredded Cheddar cheese

1. Brown ground beef in a large Dutch oven over medium-high heat, stirring constantly, 8 to 10 minutes or until meat crumbles and is no longer pink; drain. Return to Dutch oven.

2. Stir pinto beans, next 8 ingredients, and 2 cups water into beef; bring to a boil. Reduce heat to medium-low. Simmer, stirring occasionally, 30 minutes. Serve with desired toppings.

*1½ cups chicken broth may be substituted.

Pair this soup with quesadillas, and score big points with tailgate fans.

Peppered Beef Soup

MAKES: 12 cups | **HANDS-ON TIME:** 15 min. | **TOTAL TIME:** 7 hr., 8 min.

- 1   (4-lb.) sirloin tip beef roast
- ½   cup all-purpose flour
- 2   Tbsp. canola oil
- 1   medium-size red onion, thinly sliced
- 6   garlic cloves, minced
- 2   large baking potatoes, peeled and diced
- 1   (16-oz.) package baby carrots
- 2   (12-oz.) bottles lager beer*
- 2   Tbsp. balsamic vinegar
- 2   Tbsp. Worcestershire sauce
- 2   Tbsp. dried parsley flakes
- 1   Tbsp. beef bouillon granules
- 1½ to 3 tsp. freshly ground pepper
- 4   bay leaves

1. Rinse roast, and pat dry. Cut a 1-inch-deep cavity in the shape of an "X" on top of roast. (Do not cut all the way through roast.) Dredge roast in all-purpose flour; shake off excess.

2. Cook roast in hot oil in a Dutch oven over medium-high heat 1 to 2 minutes on each side or until lightly browned.

3. Place roast in a 6-qt. slow cooker. Stuff cavity with sliced red onion and minced garlic; top roast with potatoes and baby carrots. Pour beer, balsamic vinegar, and Worcestershire sauce into slow cooker. Sprinkle with parsley, bouillon, and ground pepper. Add bay leaves to liquid in slow cooker.

4. Cover and cook on LOW 7 to 8 hours or until fork-tender. Discard bay leaves. Shred roast using two forks. Season with salt to taste.

*3 cups low-sodium beef broth may be substituted.

John's Red Beans & Rice

MAKES: 10 to 12 servings | **HANDS-ON TIME:** 30 min. | **TOTAL TIME:** 3 hr., 55 min.

Devour the competition with this Creole dish to satisfy even the hungriest Tiger. Serve over hot cooked rice.

1 (16-oz.) package dried red kidney beans
1 lb. mild smoked sausage, cut into ¼-inch-thick slices
1 (½-lb.) smoked ham hock, cut in half
¼ cup vegetable oil
3 celery ribs, diced
1 medium-size yellow onion, diced
1 green bell pepper, diced
3 bay leaves
3 garlic cloves, chopped
2 Tbsp. salt-free Cajun seasoning
1 tsp. kosher salt
1 tsp. dried thyme
1 tsp. ground pepper
3 (32-oz.) containers low-sodium chicken broth
Hot cooked rice

1. Place beans in a large Dutch oven; add water 2 inches above beans. Bring to a boil. Boil 1 minute; cover, remove from heat, and let stand 1 hour. Drain.

2. Cook sausage and ham in hot oil in Dutch oven over medium-high heat 8 to 10 minutes or until browned. Drain sausage and ham on paper towels, reserving 2 Tbsp. drippings in Dutch oven. Add celery and next 8 ingredients to hot drippings; cook over low heat, stirring occasionally, 15 minutes.

3. Add broth, beans, sausage, and ham to Dutch oven. Bring to a simmer. Cook, stirring occasionally, 2 hours or until beans are tender. Discard ham hock and bay leaves. Serve over hot cooked rice.

Beef Vegetable Soup

MAKES: 18 cups | **HANDS-ON TIME:** 15 min. | **TOTAL TIME:** 1 hr., 20 min.

Beef Vegetable Soup is the ultimate comfort food to help keep you warm on a chilly fall night before or after kickoff.

1½ lb. beef stew meat
1 Tbsp. olive oil
1 (32-oz.) bag frozen mixed vegetables (peas, carrots, green beans, and lima beans)
1 (15-oz.) can tomato sauce
1 (14.5-oz.) can Italian-style diced tomatoes
1 medium-size baking potato, peeled and diced
1 celery rib, chopped
1 medium onion, chopped
2 garlic cloves, minced
½ cup ketchup
1 extra-large chicken bouillon cube
½ tsp. pepper

1. Cook meat in hot oil in a large Dutch oven over medium-high heat 6 to 8 minutes or until browned.

2. Stir in frozen mixed vegetables, next 9 ingredients, and 1½ qt. water, stirring to loosen particles from bottom of Dutch oven. Bring mixture to a boil over medium-high heat; cover, reduce heat to low, and simmer, stirring occasionally, 55 to 60 minutes or until potatoes are tender.

Note: We tested with Knorr Chicken Bouillon cube.

John's Red Beans & Rice

GEAUX
Tigers®

Gumbo. Jambalaya. Fried catfish. Red beans and rice. The flavors and traditions of South Louisiana spice up the tailgating at LSU® and guarantee that no matter what happens on the field, friends and foes alike head home fat and happy.

Hours, sometimes days, before kickoff, fanatic followers of the purple and gold flood Baton Rouge and settle in for a raucous good time. What you'll find here is a microcosm of Bayou culture—part Mardi Gras, part frat party, part family reunion.

Huge motor homes crank up booming sound systems. Sports fans gather around big-screen TVs broadcasting afternoon football games. Home cooks and professional caterers alike stir giant pots full of Louisiana favorites, from étouffée to alligator sauce piquante. All of this plays out against the backdrop of LSU's magnificent moss-draped live oaks and red-tiled buildings.

By the time The Golden Band from Tigerland marches across campus and struts into Tiger Stadium playing their jazzy Pregame Salute, fans are in a frenzy and ready for a football game. "I am telling you, this is the moment every LSU fan lives for," says one Louisiana native.

The Tigers rarely lose when they play at home—there's a reason they call their stadium Death Valley. But win or lose, festivities continue long into the night all across the state's capital city. As they say in Louisiana, *"Laissez les bon temps roulez!"* Let the good times roll!

The LSU Tiger Marching Band is regarded as one of the top college marching bands in the country. Fans agree that all the memories of more than 100 football seasons would not be as special were it not for the talented Golden Band from Tigerland.

Baton Rouge, LA

Mike the Tiger™ may well be the
most famous man in Louisiana.

Mike VI, the current mascot, has reigned over the LSU® campus since 2007, but the tiger's tale began more than 75 years ago, on October 21, 1936, when Mike I, LSU's first live tiger mascot, arrived on campus.

A sleek Siberian-Bengal tiger lies on a carpet of green grass, basking in the hot Louisiana sun. Except for the lazy flipping of his tail and an occasional growl, the big cat appears blissfully unaware of the throng of admirers gathered on the other side of the fence.

"I always bring my friends to see Mike when we come to Baton Rouge," says graduate Jennie Verner. "He's a pretty big deal around here."

Mike the Tiger, the school's official mascot, lives in the shadow of Tiger Stadium on the Baton Rouge campus, where he's coddled and spied upon with an intensity befitting his celebrity status. His posh living quarters include a man-made stream, splashing waterfall, and bathing pool. Just before home games, Mike is trucked to Tiger Stadium in his custom trailer and parked just outside the visitors' dressing room. During the pre-game show, he is wheeled slowly around the field with the pomp of a homecoming queen.

Giant Oaks, Weepy Spanish Moss

Though Baton Rouge is a sizeable city and home to the state capitol, life here seems to revolve around LSU and its Tigers. The university is one of the most beautiful parts of the city, with its man-made lakes and Italianate architecture. "The campus is absolutely breathtaking," Jennie gushes. "Giant oak trees coated with Spanish moss create a canopy covering nearly every inch of the campus, and the buildings are all topped with terra-cotta tile."

Tame a Tiger-Size Appetite

One of the main entertainment districts for students and fans sits just outside the **North Gates** of campus. Here, **Louie's Café**, a 24-hour diner, offers round-the-clock breakfast, and **The Chimes** wows with its Acadian-inspired menu and arm-long list of beers from around the world. "Louisianans are a hard group to impress when it comes to good food, but The Chimes is everyone's favorite spot to eat and imbibe," Jennie explains. "I love their eggs Benedict topped with fried crawfish and mimosas in pint glasses."

Still, if there's one place that defines Baton Rouge, it's the **Pastime**, located a block from the river under I-10. Customers scribble their names and orders on scraps of paper and pick up their food when called. Some swear by the spicy boudin pizza, but

The Chimes

the roast beef po'boys are legendary. "It's the consummate hole in the wall, but I love it," says Brit Huckabay. "I used to have a professor who put the Pastime on every exam. You had to know how to spell it to graduate."

Chelsea's Café is a funky, laid-back bistro that sits under the Perkins Road Underpass. There's an outdoor patio and live music several nights a week. Fans rave about the chicken-fried chicken, but first-timers should try the six-cheese grilled cheese on focaccia and homemade tomato-basil soup.

George's restaurant claims several locations and is a favorite for ¾-pound burgers, onion rings, and shrimp po'boys. **Acme Oyster House** serves its po'boys with hot sauce-infused mayonnaise on request, while **Sammy's Grill** is noted for its gumbo and boiled crawfish in season. Real football fans will want to stop by **T.J. Ribs** for barbecue and a peek at Billy Cannon's Heisman Trophy, part of the restaurant's memorabilia collection.

On campus, the **LSU AgCenter Dairy Store** sells ice cream and cheese made from milk supplied by LSU cows, as well as sandwiches and snacks. Tiger Bite is the store's signature scoop—a rich, golden vanilla with a blueberry swirl. Dairy

Old State Capitol

Store ice cream is also sold inside the stadium.

Exploring History

Visitors can walk, run, or bike the paths that hug the shores of the **LSU Lakes.** Downtown, both the old and new **State Capitols** welcome history buffs, as does the USS *Kidd*, a WWII-era Navy destroyer. Those traveling toward New Orleans with time to spare must take time to explore the **Great Mississippi River Road** for antebellum homes, lush gardens, and beautiful scenery.

For more information: **Baton Rouge Area Convention & Visitors Bureau, 800/527-6843** or **225/383-1825.**

LSU Tigers® Menu

Chicken-and-Sausage Gumbo
(recipe below)

Creole Potato Salad (page 192)

Muffuletta Dip (page 86)

**Bayou Fried Shrimp
with Rémoulade Sauce** (page 134)

Pecan Pralines (page 210)

A symbol of Creole cooking, gumbo is ubiquitous in homes, restaurants, and tailgates across Louisiana. Andouille sausage makes this recipe a classic and, as in any good gumbo, a richly colored roux thickens the stew.

Chicken-and-Sausage Gumbo

MAKES: 4 to 6 servings | **HANDS-ON TIME:** 55 min. | **TOTAL TIME:** 3 hr., 55 min.

1	lb. andouille sausage, cut into ¼-inch-thick slices	2	qt. hot water
4	skinned, bone-in chicken breasts	3	garlic cloves, minced
		2	bay leaves
Vegetable oil		1	Tbsp. Worcestershire sauce
¾	cup all-purpose flour	2	tsp. Creole seasoning
1	medium onion, chopped	½	tsp. dried thyme
½	green bell pepper, chopped	½	to 1 tsp. hot sauce
2	celery ribs, sliced	4	green onions, sliced
		Hot cooked rice	

1. Cook sausage in a Dutch oven over medium heat, stirring constantly, 5 minutes or until browned. Drain on paper towels, reserving drippings in Dutch oven.

2. Cook chicken in hot drippings over medium heat 5 minutes or until browned. Transfer to paper towels, reserving drippings in Dutch oven.

3. Add enough oil to drippings in Dutch oven to measure ½ cup. Add flour, and cook over medium heat, stirring constantly, 20 to 25 minutes or until roux is chocolate colored.

4. Stir in onion, bell pepper, and celery; cook, stirring often, 8 minutes or until tender. Gradually add 2 qt. hot water, and bring mixture to a boil; add chicken, garlic, and next 5 ingredients. Reduce heat to low, and simmer, stirring occasionally, 1 hour. Remove chicken; let cool (about 45 minutes).

5. Add sausage to gumbo; cook 30 minutes. Stir in green onions; cook 30 more minutes.

6. Bone chicken, and cut meat into strips; return chicken to gumbo, and simmer 5 minutes. Remove and discard bay leaves. Serve over hot cooked rice.

LSU has a rich football heritage. Their first football game in school history was played on November 25, 1893. This photo was taken with the team of 1901.

Smoky Red Pepper Soup

MAKES: 8 cups | **HANDS-ON TIME:** 30 min. | **TOTAL TIME:** 1 hr., 25 min., including pistou

- 3   Tbsp. butter
- 6   large red bell peppers, chopped
- 3   medium carrots, chopped
- 1   large sweet onion, diced
- 2   garlic cloves, minced
- 3   Tbsp. tomato paste
- 1   Tbsp. finely grated fresh ginger
- 2   tsp. smoked paprika
- 1   tsp. ground coriander
- 5   cups vegetable broth
- 2   bay leaves
- ¼   cup whipping cream

Collard Green Pistou

1. Melt butter in a large Dutch oven over medium-high heat; add bell peppers and next 2 ingredients. Sauté 12 to 15 minutes or until onion is golden. Stir in garlic and next 4 ingredients. Cook, stirring constantly, 2 minutes.

2. Add broth and bay leaves; bring to a boil. Reduce heat to medium-low, and simmer, stirring often, 25 minutes or until vegetables are tender. Discard bay leaves.

3. Process soup with a handheld blender until smooth. Stir in cream, and season with salt and pepper to taste. Cook over medium heat 10 minutes or until thoroughly heated. Serve with Collard Green Pistou.

Note: If you don't have a handheld blender, let mixture cool slightly after Step 2; process mixture, in batches, in a regular blender until smooth. Return mixture to Dutch oven, and proceed with recipe as directed in Step 3.

Collard Green Pistou

MAKES: 1 cup | **HANDS-ON TIME:** 15 min. | **TOTAL TIME:** 15 min.

- 2   cups firmly packed chopped fresh collard greens
- 2   garlic cloves
- ⅔   cup extra virgin olive oil
- ¼   tsp. dried crushed red pepper
- 2   tsp. lemon zest
- 1   Tbsp. fresh lemon juice
- ¾   tsp. salt
- ¼   tsp. pepper

1. Cook collard greens in boiling salted water to cover 4 to 6 minutes or until tender; drain. Plunge into ice water to stop the cooking process; drain well. Process garlic in a food processor until finely ground. Add greens, olive oil, and red pepper; process 2 to 3 seconds or until finely chopped. Stir in remaining ingredients.

This pesto partners well with ciabatta or sourdough and makes a great sandwich spread.

Extra Point: You can run the option, so make a substitution if you'd like to—kale, turnip, or mustard greens for collard greens.

Smoky Red Pepper Soup

Basil Tomato Soup

MAKES: 15 cups | **HANDS-ON TIME:** 20 min. | **TOTAL TIME:** 1 hr.

A tastier take on a creamy classic, this recipe takes tomato soup to the next level with fried okra and fresh basil.

2 medium onions, chopped
4 Tbsp. olive oil, divided
3 (35-oz.) cans Italian-style whole peeled tomatoes with basil
1 (32-oz.) container chicken broth
1 cup loosely packed fresh basil leaves
3 garlic cloves
1 tsp. lemon zest
1 Tbsp. fresh lemon juice
1 tsp. salt
1 tsp. sugar
½ tsp. pepper
1 (16-oz.) package frozen breaded cut okra

1. Sauté onions in 2 Tbsp. hot oil in a large Dutch oven over medium-high heat 9 to 10 minutes or until tender. Add tomatoes and chicken broth. Bring to a boil, reduce heat to medium-low, and simmer, stirring occasionally, 20 minutes. Process mixture with a handheld blender until smooth.

2. Process basil, next 4 ingredients, ¼ cup water, and remaining 2 Tbsp. oil in a food processor until smooth, stopping to scrape down sides. Stir basil mixture, sugar, and pepper into soup. Cook 10 minutes or until thoroughly heated.

3. Meanwhile, cook okra according to package directions. Serve with soup.

Loaded Potato Soup

MAKES: 8 servings | **HANDS-ON TIME:** 15 min. | **TOTAL TIME:** 3 hr., 35 min.

4 lb. new potatoes, peeled and cut into ¼-inch-thick slices
1 small onion, chopped
2 (14-oz.) cans chicken broth
2 tsp. salt
½ tsp. pepper
1 pt. half-and-half
Toppings: shredded Cheddar cheese, crumbled bacon, green onion slices

1. Layer sliced potatoes in a lightly greased 6-qt. slow cooker; top with chopped onion.

2. Stir together chicken broth, salt, and pepper; pour over potatoes and onion. (Broth will not completely cover potatoes and onion.) Cover and cook on HIGH 3 to 5 hours or until potatoes are tender. Mash mixture with a potato masher; stir in half-and-half. Cover and cook on HIGH 20 more minutes or until mixture is thoroughly heated. Ladle into bowls, and serve with desired toppings.

Chunky Beef Chili

MAKES: 9 cups | **HANDS-ON TIME:** 38 min. | **TOTAL TIME:** 2 hr., 18 min.

4   lb. boneless chuck roast, cut into ½-inch pieces
2   Tbsp. chili powder
2   (6-oz.) cans tomato paste
1   (32-oz.) container beef broth
2   (8-oz.) cans tomato sauce
2   tsp. granulated garlic
1   tsp. salt
1   tsp. onion powder
1   tsp. ground oregano
1   tsp. ground cumin
1   tsp. paprika
½   tsp. ground black pepper
¼   tsp. ground red pepper
Toppings: crushed tortilla chips, sour cream, shredded Cheddar cheese, chopped onion

1. Cook meat, in batches, in a Dutch oven over medium-high heat, stirring occasionally, 8 to 10 minutes or until browned on all sides. Remove meat, reserving drippings in Dutch oven. Add chili powder to Dutch oven; cook, stirring constantly, 2 minutes. Stir in tomato paste; cook 5 minutes.
2. Return beef to Dutch oven. Stir in beef broth and next 9 ingredients; bring to a boil over medium-high heat. Reduce heat to low, and simmer, stirring occasionally, 1½ hours or until beef is tender. Serve with Buttermilk Cornbread (page 174), if desired, and desired toppings.

This hearty beef chili features boneless chuck roast and a medley of traditional seasonings. Serve with Buttermilk Cornbread (page 174).

Game-Day Chili

MAKES: 8 to 10 servings | **HANDS-ON TIME:** 15 min. | **TOTAL TIME:** 2 hr., 30 min.

2   lb. ground chuck
1   medium onion, chopped
3   to 4 garlic cloves, minced
2   Tbsp. chili powder
2   tsp. ground cumin
1   to 2 tsp. ground red pepper
1   tsp. paprika
1   (6-oz.) can tomato paste
2   (15-oz.) cans pinto beans, drained and rinsed
1   (14.5-oz.) can beef broth
1   (12-oz.) bottle dark beer
3   (8-oz.) cans tomato sauce
1   (4.5-oz.) can chopped green chiles, undrained
1   Tbsp. Worcestershire sauce

1. Brown first 3 ingredients in a 5- to 6-qt. Dutch oven over medium heat, stirring occasionally, 8 to 10 minutes or until meat crumbles and is no longer pink. Drain well, and return to Dutch oven. Add chili powder and next 3 ingredients; cook 1 minute. Add tomato paste, and cook 1 minute. Add remaining ingredients. Bring to a boil. Cover, reduce heat to low, and simmer 2 hours.

Super-Quick Chili

MAKES: 8 servings | **HANDS-ON TIME:** 10 min. | **TOTAL TIME:** 30 min.

2	lb. lean ground beef
2	Tbsp. chili powder
1	Tbsp. Creole seasoning
1	tsp. ground cumin
2	(16-oz.) cans diced tomatoes with green peppers and onion
2	(16-oz.) cans small red beans
2	(8-oz.) cans tomato sauce

Toppings: shredded Cheddar cheese, sliced green onions, diced tomatoes

1. Brown beef in a Dutch oven over medium-high heat, stirring often, 6 to 8 minutes or until beef crumbles and is no longer pink; drain well. Return beef to Dutch oven; sprinkle with chili powder, Creole seasoning, and cumin, and sauté 1 minute.

2. Stir in diced tomatoes and next 2 ingredients, and bring to a boil over medium-high heat, stirring occasionally. Cover, reduce heat to low, and simmer, stirring occasionally, 15 minutes. Serve with toppings.

 Extra Point: This chili is delicious as a hot dog topper, over nachos, or with a simple wedge of cornbread.

Tortilla Turkey Soup

MAKES: 8 cups | **HANDS-ON TIME:** 30 min. | **TOTAL TIME:** 40 min.

10	(6-inch) fajita-size corn tortillas, cut into ½-inch-wide strips and divided
	Vegetable cooking spray
1	small onion, chopped
2	garlic cloves, chopped
1	small jalapeño pepper, seeded and minced
1	Tbsp. olive oil
1	(32-oz.) container chicken broth
1	(10-oz.) can medium enchilada sauce
2	cups chopped cooked turkey
1	tsp. ground cumin

Toppings: chopped avocado, shredded sharp Cheddar cheese, chopped fresh cilantro, chopped tomatoes

1. Preheat oven to 450°. Place half of tortilla strips in a single layer on a baking sheet. Coat strips with cooking spray; bake 10 minutes or until browned and crisp, stirring once.

2. Sauté onion and next 2 ingredients in hot olive oil in a Dutch oven over medium-high heat 5 to 6 minutes or until browned.

3. Add chicken broth and remaining unbaked tortilla strips to onion mixture. Cook broth mixture over medium heat 3 to 5 minutes or until tortilla strips soften and broth mixture thickens slightly.

4. Stir in enchilada sauce and next 2 ingredients, and cook 6 to 8 minutes or until mixture is thoroughly heated. (Do not boil.) Serve with baked tortilla strips and desired toppings.

Rotisserie chicken will work in a pinch—simply make a substitution for the turkey.

Super-Quick Chili

Chicken-and-Brisket Brunswick Stew

MAKES: 16 cups | **HANDS-ON TIME:** 20 min. | **TOTAL TIME:** 2 hr., 40 min.

- 2 large onions, chopped
- 2 garlic cloves, minced
- 1 Tbsp. vegetable oil
- 1½ Tbsp. jarred beef soup base
- 2 lb. skinned and boned chicken breasts
- 1 (28-oz.) can fire-roasted crushed tomatoes
- 1 (12-oz.) package frozen white shoepeg or whole kernel corn
- 1 (10-oz.) package frozen cream-style corn, thawed
- 1 (9-oz.) package frozen baby lima beans
- 1 (12-oz.) bottle chili sauce
- 1 Tbsp. brown sugar
- 1 Tbsp. yellow mustard
- 1 Tbsp. Worcestershire sauce
- ½ tsp. coarsely ground pepper
- 1 lb. chopped barbecued beef brisket (without sauce)
- 1 Tbsp. fresh lemon juice
- Hot sauce (optional)

1. Sauté onions and garlic in hot oil in a 7.5-qt. Dutch oven over medium-high heat 3 to 5 minutes or until tender.

2. Stir together beef soup base and 2 cups water, and add to Dutch oven. Stir in chicken and next 9 ingredients. Bring to a boil. Cover, reduce heat to low, and cook, stirring occasionally, 2 hours.

3. Uncover and shred chicken into large pieces using two forks. Stir in brisket and lemon juice. Cover and cook 10 minutes. Serve with hot sauce, if desired.

Note: We tested with Superior Touch Better Than Bouillon Beef Base and Muir Glen Organic Fire Roasted Crushed Tomatoes.

Get a head start on tailgating season by preparing and freezing this hearty stew up to one month ahead. Thaw it in the refrigerator overnight, and reheat it over medium heat just before kickoff.

Mississippi State cheerleaders chant on the sidelines during a home game in 1980.

A TALE OF

Cowbells

Like Joshua at the Battle of Jericho,
Mississippi State fans understand
the power of musical intimidation.
A handful of State fanatics furiously shaking
their infamous cowbells can sound
like an army of thousands.

School legend says fans adopted the tradition in the '30s after a Jersey cow wearing a bell around her neck wandered onto the field during a Mississippi State vs. Ole Miss game. State pummeled their archrivals that day, and the cowbell became a good luck charm.

Now an enduring symbol of school spirit and pride, the cowbell tradition is unrivaled in college sports. "It's our one and only unique tradition, and we hold it close to our hearts," a recent alum explains. "I retired my first cowbell when I graduated. I want to give it to my kid to carry on the tradition."

Ah, but there was one little fly in the ointment for State fans. Rivals complained that all that racket gave the Maroon and White an unfair advantage, prompting the SEC to ban artificial noisemakers in 1974. Undeterred, defiant Bulldog fans smuggled their contraband cowbells into stadiums near and far and rang them with a deafening fervor.

In 2010, conference presidents and athletic directors relented and passed the "Cowbell Clause." Fans can shake their bells only at "appropriate times" or the school may be fined. There's even a Web site designed to teach cowbell etiquette: www.respectthebell.com.

Mississippi State fans hear
pride in cowbell clank.

Starkville, MS

Throughout history, Mississippi State has been known as "The People's University."

True to its name, the Chapel of Memories is a popular site for weddings, receptions, and campus ceremonies.

Mississippi State fans are a passionate lot. Ask them to name a favorite spot on campus, and the debate could go on for days.

Some pick the Drill Field, the university's main quadrangle, while others vote for the Chapel of Memories, built with bricks salvaged from the original campus building that burned in 1959. Rabid football fans declare Davis Wade Stadium the true heart of campus, while baseball junkies claim it's the Left Field Lounge at Dudy Noble Field.

The Junction

But mention **The Junction** and all debate stops. It's pretty. It's new. It nods to the school's history as a rail stop and unravels a modern traffic snarl. Best of all, the pedestrian-friendly green space provides a perfect spot for tailgating. What's not to love?

"Tailgating really took off at Mississippi State when The Junction was built," says recent graduate Kevin Martin. "They took out a 5-way stop that was a nightmare and replaced it with trees, grass, and flowers. It was a huge step in making our university an even better environment on game days."

The Consummate College Town

But Bulldog fans don't really need another excuse to visit. They're unapologetically partisan—about their school and its hometown of less than 25,000 souls. Starkville is a college town in the truest sense of the word. The university is the largest employer in town, and locally owned businesses and restaurants do a brisk business with the MSU crowd.

Adjacent to campus, **The Cotton District** is without a doubt the most popular place for college students to live and play. Builder Dan Camp continues to transform the neighborhood with classical architecture styles, bright colors, and inviting streetscapes. "By accident, I started investing in a rundown area of town soon after I graduated from college," Dan explains. "Any damn fool could see it was right by the university and would someday take off. We've succeeded in making this a beautiful, walkable neighborhood where students want to be."

Big Screen TVs and Wings

City Bagel Cafe serves the obvious fresh-baked bagels, but it's a popular spot for lunch every day and dinner three nights a week. A bonafide sports bar, **StaggerIn Sports Grill** offers big screen TVs, wings, and po'boys, while **Rock Bottom Bar & Grill** serves sliders and hoagies. With a brick patio out front, **Bin 612** is a perfect spot for people watching.

Locals debate the merits of the town's best pizzerias and know to call

Oby's

ahead when ordering the deep-dish Chicago stuffed pie at **Dave's Dark Horse Tavern**. At **Stromboli's** on University, thin-crust pizzas are served with a side of sauce to dip the crust in. There's no debate, however, when it comes to the New Orleans-style po'boys and muffulettas at **Oby's**, a Starkville original.

Mississippi-born Ty Thames is the local celebrity chef with four restaurants under his belt. He cures and smokes his own meats and sources many of his ingredients from local farmers. Downtown, **Restaurant Tyler** serves the flavors of the South, from fried chicken and Delta catfish to purple hull peas and turnip greens.

Starkvegas Classics

To founders Barry and Margaret Ann Woods, "a little dooey" is defined as a gathering of friends and family. Now their barbecue restaurant, **The Little Dooey**, is a classic in Starkville. Locals say the fried catfish is the best for miles around.

Longtime State fans make a stop at the **MSU Cheese Store** before leaving town. The school's Dairy Science students have been making and selling cheese from the university's own dairy herd since 1938. The MSU Cheese Store opens weekdays and for home games.

For more information: **Starkville Convention & Visitors Bureau, 800/ 649-8687** or **662/ 323-3322**.

Stromboli's

Mississippi State Bulldogs™ Menu

Buttermilk Cornbread (page 174) or
Sour Cream Cornbread (page 176)

Vegetarian Black Bean Chili (recipe below)
or Super-Quick Chili (page 120) or
White Lightning Chicken Chili (page 130)

From-Scratch Oven Fries (page 84)

Mississippi Mud Cookies
(page 222)

Vegetarian Black Bean Chili

MAKES: 10 cups | **HANDS-ON TIME:** 20 min. | **TOTAL TIME:** 55 min.

With vegetarian burger crumbles, this meatless main dish is packed with flavor and substance. Serve with your favorite chili toppers.

3 (15.5-oz.) cans black beans, divided
1 large sweet onion, chopped
3 garlic cloves, minced
2 Tbsp. vegetable oil
4 tsp. chili powder
1 tsp. ground cumin
½ tsp. pepper
¼ tsp. salt
2 (14.5-oz.) cans petite diced tomatoes with jalapeño peppers
1 (12-oz.) package meatless burger crumbles
1 extra-large vegetable bouillon cube
Toppings: sour cream, shredded Cheddar cheese, sliced pickled jalapeño peppers, diced tomatoes

1. Drain and rinse 2 cans black beans. (Do not drain third can.)
2. Sauté onion and garlic in hot oil in a large Dutch oven over medium-high heat 6 to 8 minutes or until tender. Stir in chili powder and next 3 ingredients; sauté 3 minutes. Stir in diced tomatoes, next 2 ingredients, drained and undrained beans, and 2 cups water. Bring to a boil over medium-high heat; reduce heat to medium-low, and simmer, stirring occasionally, 30 minutes. Serve chili with desired toppings.

Meaty Black Bean Chili: Omit vegetable oil. Substitute 1 lb. lean ground beef for crumbles. Prepare recipe as directed, sautéing ground beef with onion and garlic in Step 2 for 10 minutes or until meat crumbles and is no longer pink. Proceed as directed.

No need to call a
time-out! Use
rotisserie chicken
to prepare this
recipe in a flash.

White Lightning Chicken Chili

MAKES: 11½ cups | **HANDS-ON TIME:** 30 min. | **TOTAL TIME:** 40 min., including salsa

1   **large sweet onion, diced**
2   **garlic cloves, minced**
2   **Tbsp. olive oil**
4   **cups shredded cooked chicken**
2   **(14½-oz.) cans chicken broth**
2   **(4.5-oz.) cans chopped green chiles**
1   **(1.25-oz.) package white chicken chili seasoning mix**
3   **(16-oz.) cans navy beans**
**Toppings: sour cream, shredded Monterey Jack cheese, fresh cilantro leaves,
     Avocado-Mango Salsa**

1. Sauté onion and garlic in hot oil in a large Dutch oven over medium-high heat 5 minutes or until onion is tender. Stir in chicken, next 3 ingredients, and 2 cans navy beans. Coarsely mash remaining can of navy beans, and stir into chicken mixture. Bring to a boil, stirring often; cover, reduce heat to medium-low, and simmer, stirring occasionally, 10 minutes. Serve with desired toppings.
Note: We tested with McCormick White Chicken Chili Seasoning Mix.

Avocado-Mango Salsa

MAKES: about 2 cups | **HANDS-ON TIME:** 10 min. | **TOTAL TIME:** 10 min.

1   **large avocado, cubed**
1   **cup diced fresh mango**
⅓   **cup diced red onion**
2   **Tbsp. chopped fresh cilantro**
2   **Tbsp. fresh lime juice**

1. Stir together all ingredients. Serve immediately.

 Extra Point: Avocado-Mango Salsa stands alone as an appetizer with your favorite chips, or serve this salsa as a topping on your favorite white chili as we did.

Bully, a member of the cheerleading team, assists in rallying the fans at games and pep rallies. Hail, dear ol' State!

White Lightning Chicken Chili

Slow-Cooked BBQ Chicken
Sandwiches, page 166

(6)
HOT PROSPECTS

Fire up the grill, and get your main dish on, tailgate style. Whether it's burgers, steak, BBQ, or chicken, there's something for everyone no matter which team you love.

Lowcountry Boil

MAKES: 6 servings | **HANDS-ON TIME:** 10 min. | **TOTAL TIME:** 5 hr., 40 min.

12	small new potatoes (1¼ lb.)	½	(12-count) package frozen corn on the cob (do not thaw)
1	(12-oz.) can beer	2	lb. unpeeled, large raw shrimp (26/30 count)
4	to 5 Tbsp. Old Bay seasoning		Cocktail sauce
2	celery ribs, cut into 4-inch pieces		
1	onion, quartered		
2	lemons, halved		
1	lb. kielbasa sausage, cut into 1-inch pieces		

1. Place potatoes in a 7-qt. slow cooker. Add 10 cups water, beer, and next 3 ingredients. Squeeze juice from lemon halves into mixture in slow cooker; add lemon halves to slow cooker. Cover and cook on LOW 3 hours.

2. Add sausage and corn. Cover and cook on LOW 2 hours. Add shrimp; stir gently. Cover and cook on HIGH 15 minutes or just until shrimp turn pink. Turn off slow cooker; let stand 15 minutes. Drain. Serve with cocktail sauce.

Bayou Fried Shrimp

MAKES: 6 to 8 servings | **HANDS-ON TIME:** 30 min. | **TOTAL TIME:** 1 hr., 50 min., including sauce

3	lb. unpeeled, large raw shrimp (26/30 count)	1	tsp. Cajun seasoning
2	cups milk	1	(12-oz.) package fish fry mix
1	large egg	1	Tbsp. Cajun seasoning
1	Tbsp. yellow mustard		Vegetable oil
			Rémoulade Sauce

1. Peel shrimp, leaving tails on. Butterfly shrimp by making a deep slit down back of each from large end to tail, cutting to but not through inside curve of shrimp. Devein shrimp, and place in a large bowl.

2. Whisk together milk and next 3 ingredients. Pour mixture over shrimp. Let stand 15 minutes to 1 hour.

3. Combine fish fry mix and 1 Tbsp. Cajun seasoning. Remove shrimp from marinade, discarding marinade. Dredge shrimp in fish fry mixture, and shake off excess. Arrange on baking sheets.

4. Pour oil to depth of 3 inches into a Dutch oven; heat to 325°. Fry shrimp, in batches, 1½ minutes on each side or until golden brown; drain on wire racks over paper towels. Serve with Rémoulade Sauce.

Note: We tested with Zatarain's Wonderful Fish-Fri and Walker & Sons Slap Ya Mama Cajun Seasoning.

Use a large paper grocery sack to toss shrimp with fish fry mix and Cajun seasoning.

Rémoulade Sauce

MAKES: 2 cups | **HANDS-ON TIME:** 5 min. | **TOTAL TIME:** 1 hr., 5 min.

1½	cups mayonnaise	1½	Tbsp. fresh lemon juice
4	green onions, sliced	1	garlic clove, pressed
3	Tbsp. chopped fresh parsley	1½	tsp. refrigerated horseradish
3	Tbsp. Creole mustard	1	tsp. paprika

1. Stir together all ingredients; cover and chill 1 hour.

Lowcountry Boil

Nix the buns and make tacos by stuffing warm corn tortillas with fried fish, slaw or shredded cabbage, cilantro, Pico de Gallo (page 93), and cheese.

Fried Fish Sandwiches

MAKES: 4 servings | **HANDS-ON TIME:** 30 min. | **TOTAL TIME:** 30 min.

2	lb. grouper, mahi-mahi, cod, or halibut fillets	2	tsp. baking powder
2	tsp. Greek seasoning, divided	2	cups cold beer
1½	tsp. salt, divided	1	large egg, lightly beaten
1	tsp. freshly ground pepper, divided		Vegetable oil
2¼	cups all-purpose flour	4	sesame seed hamburger buns
¼	cup plain yellow cornmeal		Tartar sauce or mayonnaise
		4	green leaf lettuce leaves
		4	tomato slices

1. Cut fish into 3-inch strips. Sprinkle with 1 tsp. Greek seasoning, 1 tsp. salt, and ½ tsp. pepper.

2. Combine flour, cornmeal, baking powder, and remaining 1 tsp. Greek seasoning, ½ tsp. salt, and ½ tsp. pepper; stir well. Add cold beer and egg, stirring until thoroughly blended and smooth.

3. Pour oil to depth of 2 to 3 inches into a Dutch oven; heat to 375°.

4. Dip fish strips into batter, coating both sides well; shake off excess. Fry fish, in batches, 2 minutes on each side or until golden. (Do not crowd pan.) Drain on paper towels.

5. Spread top half of each bun with tartar sauce. Place 1 lettuce leaf and 1 tomato slice on bottom half of each bun; top each with 2 fried fish strips and top halves of buns.

Poblano Fish Tacos

MAKES: 6 servings | **HANDS-ON TIME:** 20 min. | **TOTAL TIME:** 40 min.

1	large poblano pepper	4	Tbsp. olive oil, divided
½	English cucumber, coarsely chopped	1	Tbsp. mango-lime seafood seasoning
1	cup grape tomatoes, quartered	1½	lb. grouper or other firm white fish fillets
2	Tbsp. chopped red onion	12	(6-inch) fajita-size corn tortillas, warmed
1	garlic clove, minced		
½	tsp. salt		Lime wedges
3	Tbsp. fresh lime juice, divided		

1. Preheat grill to 350° to 400° (medium-high) heat. Grill pepper, covered with grill lid, 3 to 4 minutes or until pepper looks blistered, turning once. Place pepper in a large zip-top plastic freezer bag; seal and let stand 10 minutes to loosen skin. Peel pepper; remove and discard seeds. Coarsely chop.

2. Combine pepper, cucumber, next 4 ingredients, 2 Tbsp. lime juice, and 2 Tbsp. olive oil in a bowl.

3. Whisk together seafood seasoning and remaining 1 Tbsp. lime juice and 2 Tbsp. olive oil in a large shallow dish or zip-top plastic freezer bag; add fish, turning to coat. Cover or seal, and chill 5 minutes, turning once. Remove fish from marinade, discarding marinade.

4. Grill fish, covered with grill lid, 3 to 4 minutes on each side or just until fish begins to flake with a fork. Cool 5 minutes. Flake fish into bite-size pieces.

5. Serve fish and salsa in warm tortillas with lime wedges.

Note: We tested with Weber Mango Lime Seafood Seasoning.

The University of Mississippi was chartered on February 24, 1844, and it opened its doors four years later. From its first class of 80 students, it has now grown to 18,000.

Fried Fish Sandwiches

Pimiento Cheese-Bacon Burgers

Pimiento Cheese-Bacon Burgers

MAKES: 6 servings | **HANDS-ON TIME:** 30 min. | **TOTAL TIME:** 30 min.

1	**lb. ground sirloin**
1	**lb. ground chuck**
1	**tsp. salt**
½	**tsp. freshly ground pepper**
¼	**cup mixed chopped fresh herbs (such as basil, mint, and oregano)**

Hamburger buns
Toppings: pimiento cheese, cooked bacon slices, lettuce, tomato slices

1. Preheat grill to 350° to 400° (medium-high) heat. Combine first 4 ingredients gently. Stir fresh herbs into meat mixture. Shape mixture into 6 (5-inch) patties.
2. Grill, covered with grill lid, 4 to 5 minutes on each side or until beef is no longer pink in center. Serve on buns with desired toppings.

 Extra Point: Try with any of the pimiento cheese variations on page 101 for a touchdown of flavor.

Bacon-Wrapped Barbecue Burgers

MAKES: 4 servings | **HANDS-ON TIME:** 40 min. | **TOTAL TIME:** 55 min.

8	**bacon slices**
1	**(4.5-oz.) jar sliced mushrooms, drained and chopped**
½	**cup chopped Vidalia or sweet onion**
2	**tsp. olive oil**

½	**cup bottled honey barbecue sauce, divided**
1½	**lb. ground beef**
	Wooden picks
¼	**tsp. salt**
4	**sesame seed hamburger buns, toasted**

1. Arrange bacon on a paper towel-lined microwave-safe plate; cover with a paper towel. Microwave bacon at HIGH 2 minutes or until edges begin to crinkle and bacon is partially cooked.
2. Sauté mushrooms and onion in hot oil in a small nonstick skillet over medium heat 4 to 5 minutes or until tender and liquid is absorbed. Remove from heat, and stir in 2 Tbsp. barbecue sauce.
3. Preheat grill to 350° to 400° (medium-high) heat. Shape beef into 8 (5-inch) thin patties. Place 2 Tbsp. mushroom mixture in center of each of 4 patties. Top with remaining patties, pressing edges to seal. Shape into 4-inch patties. Wrap sides of each patty with 2 bacon slices, overlapping ends of each slice. Secure bacon using wooden picks. Sprinkle patties with salt. Cover and chill 10 minutes.
4. Grill patties, covered with grill lid, 5 to 6 minutes on 1 side. Turn and baste with half of remaining barbecue sauce. Grill 5 to 6 minutes or until beef is no longer pink in center. Turn and baste with remaining barbecue sauce. Remove from grill, and let stand 5 minutes. Remove wooden picks. Serve burgers on buns, and top with remaining mushroom mixture.
Note: We tested with Kraft Honey Barbecue Sauce.

With pimiento cheese and bacon, this burger combines the best of the South for a winning combination.

Get a jump start on these over-the-top burgers the night before the game. Chill stuffed and wrapped burgers up to 24 hours before grilling.

HOTTY TODDY™

The Grove™

Ole Miss® is to tailgating what Bach is to music—quite simply, the best. When the Rebels™ play at home, fans fill The Grove, a grassy, tree-shaded expanse at the heart of campus, for a game-day party unsurpassed in elegance and beauty.

The Grove is off limits until 9 o'clock Friday evening, when there's a mad dash and land grab. By Saturday morning, it resembles other tailgates around the country—a sea of navy blue, cardinal red, and bright white tents filled with rejoicing fans.

But closer inspection reveals a unique slice of Southern Americana. Fresh flowers, heirloom silver, and family china grace linen-draped tables. Kids toss footballs and race around in their Sunday best. Winsome co-eds prance about in Jimmy Choos and party dresses, escorted by young men in bow ties and seersucker. More than one love-struck swain has proposed to his sweetheart on bended knee in The Grove.

Tradition rules at the University of Mississippi. The speed limit on campus is 18 mph—Archie Manning's jersey number. The band warms up to "Hype Chorale," and Ole Miss players high-five fans in The Grove on the way to the game.

If things are not going well at Vaught-Hemingway Stadium, some Rebels punt at halftime and return to tailgating. "You'll never find more Southern hospitality than in The Grove on game day," says a brunette beauty on sky-high stilettos. "We may not win every game, but we've never lost a party!"

Ole Miss has enjoyed three national titles during its football history. Some of its most notable players include Archie and Eli Manning, Charlie Conerly, and Michael Oher.

Oxford, MS

Ole Miss® is one of those places that is more than merely the sum of its parts.

Every red-blooded Ole Miss student has a picture taken beneath the Walk of Champions arch at least once during his or her stay here.

University of Mississippi students and alumni mince no words when it comes to their beloved Oxford campus. "Ole Miss is the most beautiful campus in America," says Rebecca Bertrand without hesitation. "It still takes my breath away."

Ms. Bertrand might be biased—the Houston native served as student body president in 2006. But many others willingly validate her observations. "I love it," says sophomore Meredith Beck. "It's absolutely gorgeous. Ole Miss looks like a college campus should look."

Yes, they love The Grove on game days. The columned splendor of The Lyceum inspires. And the Circle Historic District? There's no question. It's still the heart of campus.

Students love walking in the footsteps of Faulkner, Wilkie, and Grisham and consider the Mannings part of their family (the Mannings who attended Ole Miss, that is).

The town of Oxford only sweetens the deal. The founding fathers named the settlement after the British bastion of higher education in hopes of landing the first state university. When the legislature agreed to place it here, the townspeople marched from the downtown Square to campus to lay the cornerstone of The Lyceum. Oxford and Ole Miss have been indelibly linked since that day.

Decidedly "Un-Square" Bookstore

Life here still revolves around the pretty Lafayette County Courthouse Square. The courthouse itself is still in use, but one of the most talked-about businesses here is **Square Books**, an independent bookseller in three separate buildings.

The main store showcases Southern writers and hosts an impressive lineup of book signings and special events. There's a cafe and a balcony at the main store, while **Off Square Books** features lifestyle sections, and **Square Books Jr.** caters to younger readers. The old-time **Thacker Mountain Radio** show is broadcast from Square Books every Thursday night.

Pizza, Pasta, Po'Boys & Grits

Any good Ole Miss Rebel will say dining before and after the game is reserved for The Grove, but the restaurants on the Square run a close second. For breakfast pastries, homemade granola, and coffee, locals rave about **Bottletree Bakery**. The down-home Mississippi cooking is spot-on at **Ajax Diner.**

The Creole-inspired menu at **Bouré** never disappoints with buttermilk fried onion rings, terrific burgers, and entrées such as pasta jambalaya. By day, **Proud Larry's** serves tasty pasta and hand-tossed pizza, but at night, it's the place for great live music. **Abner's Famous Chicken Tenders,** started by Ole Miss football player Abner White, is within walking distance of the Square.

James Beard Foundation Award-winning chef John Currence is almost single-handedly responsible for putting Oxford on the food map with his acclaimed **City Grocery**. Open for lunch and dinner, it's the ultimate in fine dining. His other restaurants include Bouré, Big Bad Breakfast, and the newest, Snackbar.

Oxford's Literary Lion

Of course, no visit to Oxford is complete without a visit to **Rowan Oak,** home of William Faulkner. "The white mansion stands among cedar trees not far from campus," Rebecca explains. "The grounds take you back in time. I love imagining Faulkner riding about the grounds on his horse and penning masterpieces on the walls of his home. You can't help but be inspired."

For more information: **Oxford Convention & Visitors Bureau, 800/758-9177** or **662/232-2367.**

Square Books

GOOD EATS
Ajax
DINER
AIR CONDITIONED

THE OXFORD EAGLE

SERVING LUNCH & DINNER
MON - SAT   11:30 AM 10:00 PM

Rowan Oak

Ole Miss Rebels™ Menu

Herbed Dip with Baby Vegetables (page 88)

Molasses-Balsamic Steak Kabobs
(recipe below)

Broccoli, Grape, and Pasta Salad
(page 192)

Watermelon, Mâche, and Pecan Salad (page 205)

Mississippi Mud Cake
(page 236)

Pull out the fine china and polish the silver for this swanky tailgate feast. Nothing but the best for Ole Miss® fans, who are known to have never lost a party.

Molasses-Balsamic Steak Kabobs

MAKES: 4 to 6 servings | **HANDS-ON TIME:** 38 min. | **TOTAL TIME:** 1 hr.

8	(12-inch) wooden or metal skewers	2	medium-size red onions, cut into eighths
1	(1½-lb.) boneless sirloin steak, trimmed and cut into 1½-inch pieces	2	tsp. seasoned salt
		2	tsp. pepper
4	small, firm peaches, quartered	½	cup molasses
2	medium-size green tomatoes, cut into eighths	¼	cup balsamic vinegar

1. Soak wooden skewers in water to cover 30 minutes.

2. Preheat grill to 350° to 400° (medium-high) heat. Thread steak and next 3 ingredients alternately onto skewers, leaving a ¼-inch space between pieces. Sprinkle kabobs with seasoned salt and pepper. Stir together molasses and vinegar.

3. Grill kabobs, covered with grill lid, 4 minutes on each side. Baste with half of molasses mixture, and grill 2 minutes. Turn, baste with remaining half of molasses mixture, and grill 2 more minutes or until done.

 Extra Point: These kabobs are delicious over salad greens and drizzled with balsamic vinaigrette. Tote leftovers to the office for an easy lunchbox meal.

Beef Fajitas with Pico de Gallo

MAKES: 6 servings | **HANDS-ON TIME:** 20 min. | **TOTAL TIME:** 9 hr., 50 min., including pico de gallo

Season steaks overnight to bring out their full flavor and kick-start the main meal.

1	**(8-oz.) bottle zesty Italian dressing**
3	**Tbsp. fajita seasoning**
2	**(1-lb.) flank steaks**
12	**(6-inch) fajita-size flour tortillas, warmed**

Shredded Cheddar cheese
Pico de Gallo (page 93)
Garnishes: guacamole, lime wedges

1. Combine Italian dressing and fajita seasoning in a shallow dish or zip-top plastic bag; add steak. Cover or seal, and chill 8 hours, turning occasionally. Remove steak from marinade, discarding marinade.

2. Preheat a two-sided contact indoor electric grill according to manufacturer's instructions on HIGH. Place steaks on grill rack, close lid, and grill 10 minutes (medium-rare) or to desired degree of doneness. Remove steaks, and let stand 5 minutes.

3. Cut steaks diagonally across the grain into very thin slices, and serve with tortillas, cheese, and Pico de Gallo.

Note: When using an outdoor gas or charcoal grill, grill steaks, covered with grill lid, over 350° to 400° (medium-high) heat 8 minutes. Turn and grill 5 more minutes or to desired degree of doneness. Proceed as directed. We tested with McCormick Fajita Seasoning.

Southwest Flank Steak with Salsa

MAKES: 4 to 6 servings | **HANDS-ON TIME:** 25 min. | **TOTAL TIME:** 4 hr., 25 min.

2	**Tbsp. fajita seasoning**
1	**tsp. pepper**
½	**tsp. dry mustard**
2	**Tbsp. olive oil**

1	**(1½-lb.) package flank steak (½ inch thick)**

Gator Bait (Fresh Salsa and Chips) (page 77)

1. Combine first 3 ingredients. Rub olive oil over flank steak; sprinkle with seasoning blend. Cover and chill 4 hours.

2. Preheat grill to 350° to 400° (medium-high) heat. Grill, covered with grill lid, 7 to 8 minutes on each side or to desired degree of doneness. Cut steak diagonally across grain into thin strips. Serve with salsa.

Extra Point: Layer flank steak slices on split French rolls, top with Cheddar or pepper Jack cheese, and broil until cheese melts for easy Southwestern cheesesteak sandwiches.

Sweet-and-Savory Burgers

MAKES: 8 servings | **HANDS-ON TIME:** 20 min. | **TOTAL TIME:** 4 hr., 20 min.

¼ cup soy sauce
2 Tbsp. light corn syrup
1 Tbsp. fresh lemon juice
½ tsp. ground ginger
¼ tsp. garlic powder
2 green onions, thinly sliced
2 lb. ground beef
¼ cup chili sauce
¼ cup hot red pepper jelly
8 hamburger buns, toasted
Toppings: grilled sweet onion, pineapple slices

1. Stir together first 6 ingredients. Reserve 3 Tbsp. mixture; cover and chill. Pour remaining soy sauce mixture into a shallow pan or baking dish.

2. Shape beef into 8 (½-inch-thick) patties; place in a single layer in soy sauce mixture in pan, turning to coat. Cover and chill 4 hours.

3. Preheat grill to 350° to 400° (medium-high) heat. Remove patties from marinade, discarding marinade. Grill patties, covered with grill lid, 5 minutes on each side or until beef is no longer pink in center, basting occasionally with reserved 3 Tbsp. soy sauce mixture.

4. Stir together chili sauce and jelly. Serve burgers on buns with chili sauce mixture and desired toppings.

Herb-Marinated Flank Steak

MAKES: 6 servings | **HANDS-ON TIME:** 35 min. | **TOTAL TIME:** 1 hr., 15 min.

½ small sweet onion, minced
3 garlic cloves, minced
¼ cup olive oil
2 Tbsp. chopped fresh basil
1 Tbsp. chopped fresh thyme
1 Tbsp. chopped fresh rosemary
1 tsp. salt
½ tsp. dried crushed red pepper
1¾ lb. flank steak
1 lemon, halved

1. Place first 8 ingredients in a 2-gal. zip-top plastic bag, and squeeze bag to combine. Add steak; seal bag, and chill 30 minutes to 1 hour and 30 minutes. Remove steak from marinade, discarding marinade.

2. Preheat grill to 400° to 450° (high) heat. Grill steak, covered with grill lid, 9 minutes on each side or to desired degree of doneness. Remove from grill; squeeze juice from lemon over steak. Let stand 10 minutes. Cut diagonally across the grain into thin slices.

Herb-Marinated Chicken Breasts: Substitute 1¾ lb. skinned and boned chicken breasts for flank steak. Proceed with recipe as directed, grilling chicken 7 minutes on each side or until done. Hands-on Time: 30 min.; Total Time: 1 hr., 10 min.

This flavorful flank steak doesn't need to marinate overnight to score big with football fans.

Flank Steak Sandwiches with "Go Big Blue®" Cheese

MAKES: 6 servings | **HANDS-ON TIME:** 25 min. | **TOTAL TIME:** 1 hr., 40 min., including steak

2	large sweet onions
4	Tbsp. olive oil, divided
½	tsp. salt
½	tsp. freshly ground pepper
3	red bell peppers
6	(2- to 3-oz.) ciabatta or deli rolls, split*

5	oz. soft ripened blue cheese or Brie
1½	cups loosely packed arugula
	Herb-Marinated Flank Steak (page 147)
6	Tbsp. mayonnaise

1. Preheat grill to 400° to 450° (high) heat. Cut onion into ¼-inch-thick slices. Brush with 1 Tbsp. olive oil, and sprinkle with ¼ tsp. salt and ¼ tsp. pepper. Cut bell peppers into 1-inch-wide strips. Place pepper strips in a large bowl, and drizzle with 1 Tbsp. olive oil. Sprinkle with remaining ¼ tsp. salt and ¼ tsp. pepper; toss to coat.

2. Grill onion and bell pepper strips, covered with grill lid, 7 to 10 minutes on each side or until lightly charred and tender.

3. Brush cut sides of rolls with remaining 2 Tbsp. olive oil, and grill, cut sides down, without grill lid, 1 to 2 minutes or until lightly browned and toasted.

4. Spread blue cheese on cut sides of roll bottoms; top with arugula, bell pepper strips, steak, and onion. Spread mayonnaise on cut sides of roll tops. Place roll tops, mayonnaise sides down, on top of onion, pressing lightly.
*French hamburger buns may be substituted. We tested with Publix French Hamburger Buns.
Note: We tested with Saga Classic Soft-Ripened Blue-Veined Cheese.

Herb Chicken Sandwiches: Substitute Herb-Marinated Chicken Breasts (page 147) for flank steak. Proceed with recipe as directed. Hands-on Time: 25 min.; Total Time: 1 hr., 35 min., including chicken

Herb Chicken Sandwiches with Grilled Peaches: Reduce onions to 1 and red bell peppers to 2. Cut 2 large peaches into ¼-inch-thick rounds, cutting through stem and bottom ends. Proceed with recipe as directed, grilling peach slices, covered with grill lid, over 350° to 400° (medium-high) heat 3 to 5 minutes on each side or until grill marks appear. Assemble sandwiches as directed, topping onion with peach slices. Hands-on Time: 40 min.; Total Time: 1 hr., 50 min., including chicken

Saturday, November 11, 1893, was the first time an organized football game was played by students of the University of Mississippi.

Sriracha, a chile-laced condiment, packs a powerful punch. Use this spicy sauce judiciously.

Sweet Heat Hot Dogs

MAKES: 8 servings | **HANDS-ON TIME:** 15 min. | **TOTAL TIME:** 15 min.

¾	cup mayonnaise	8	hot dogs
1	Tbsp. whole grain mustard	8	hot dog buns, toasted
1	green onion, minced	1	cup chopped sweet-hot
2	Tbsp. Asian Sriracha hot chili		pickles
	sauce	2	cups shredded red cabbage

1. Preheat grill to 350° to 400° (medium-high) heat.

2. Combine first 3 ingredients and 1 Tbsp. chili sauce in a small bowl. Brush hot dogs with remaining 1 Tbsp. chili sauce.

3. Grill hot dogs, covered with grill lid, 4 to 6 minutes or until thoroughly heated. Place hot dogs in buns, and top with mayonnaise mixture. Sprinkle with chopped pickles and shredded cabbage.

Note: We tested with Wickles Pickles and Huy Fong Sriracha Hot Chili Sauce.

Braised Beef Brisket

MAKES: 16 servings | **HANDS-ON TIME:** 15 min. | **TOTAL TIME:** 4 hr., 35 min., plus 24 hr. for chilling

2	(14.5-oz.) cans low-sodium beef broth	5	garlic cloves, chopped
1	cup low-sodium soy sauce	1	Tbsp. hickory liquid smoke (optional)
¼	cup fresh lemon juice	1	(7- to 9-lb.) beef brisket

1. Stir together first 4 ingredients and, if desired, liquid smoke in a large roasting pan. Place brisket in pan, fat side up. Spoon liquid over brisket. Cover tightly with aluminum foil, and chill 24 hours.

2. Preheat oven to 300°. Bake brisket, covered, 4 to 4½ hours or until fork-tender. Uncover and let stand 20 minutes.

3. Transfer brisket to a cutting board. Trim fat from brisket. Cut brisket across the grain into thin slices. (Or cut brisket into large pieces, and shred with two forks.) Pour pan drippings through a wire-mesh strainer into a small pitcher, discarding solids. Serve brisket with drippings.

Mixed Grill

MAKES: 8 servings | **HANDS-ON TIME:** 5 min. | **TOTAL TIME:** 30 min.

4	(1½-inch-thick) center-cut bone-in pork chops
4	(6-oz.) beef tenderloin fillets (about 2 inches thick)

1. Sprinkle pork chops and beef fillets with desired amount of salt and pepper.

2. Preheat grill to 350° to 400° (medium-high) heat. Grill chops and fillets at the same time, covered with grill lid. Grill chops 8 to 10 minutes on each side or until done. Grill fillets 8 to 10 minutes; turn fillets over, and cook 5 more minutes or to desired degree of doneness. Remove chops and fillets from grill, and let stand 5 minutes.

Sweet Heat Hot Dogs

Sweet-Hot Baby Back Ribs

MAKES: 6 servings | **HANDS-ON TIME:** 30 min. | **TOTAL TIME:** 12 hr., 25 min., including sauce

2   **Tbsp. ground ginger**
1   **tsp. salt**
1   **tsp. black pepper**
½   **tsp. dried crushed red pepper**
3   **slabs baby back pork ribs (about 5½ lb.)**
2   **limes, halved**
Sweet-Hot 'Cue Sauce

1. Combine first 4 ingredients in a small bowl.
2. Rinse and pat slabs dry. If desired, remove thin membrane from back of ribs by slicing into it with a knife and then pulling it off. (This will make ribs more tender.)
3. Rub ribs with cut sides of limes, squeezing as you rub. Massage ginger mixture into meat, covering all sides. Wrap ribs tightly with plastic wrap, and place in zip-top plastic freezer bags or a 13- x 9-inch baking dish; seal or cover, and chill 8 hours.
4. Light one side of grill, heating to 350° to 400° (medium-high) heat; leave other side unlit. Let ribs stand at room temperature 30 minutes before grilling. Remove plastic wrap. Place ribs over unlit side of grill, stacking 1 on top of the other.
5. Grill, covered with grill lid, 40 minutes. Rotate ribs, moving bottom slab to top; grill 40 minutes. Rotate again, moving bottom ribs to top; grill 40 minutes.
6. Lower grill temperature to 300° to 350° (medium) heat; place ribs side by side over unlit side of grill. Cook 30 more minutes, basting with half of Sweet-Hot 'Cue Sauce. Remove from grill; let stand 10 minutes. Serve ribs with remaining Sweet-Hot 'Cue Sauce.

Nothing can compete with this first-string rib recipe. If using a three-burner grill, light both sides, and leave the center portion off.

Sweet-Hot 'Cue Sauce

MAKES: 4 cups | **HANDS-ON TIME:** 10 min. | **TOTAL TIME:** 45 min.

2   **(10-oz.) bottles sweet chili sauce**
2   **cups ketchup**
⅓   **cup firmly packed dark brown sugar**
1   **tsp. ground ginger**
1   **tsp. pepper**
½   **tsp. dried crushed red pepper**

1. Combine all ingredients in a saucepan over medium-high heat. Bring mixture to a boil; reduce heat, and simmer 30 minutes.
Note: We tested with Maggi Taste of Asia Sweet Chili Sauce.

Ole Miss defeats Texas Christian University 14-13 in the 1956 Cotton Bowl.

Grilled Baby Back Ribs

MAKES: 6 servings | **HANDS-ON TIME:** 30 min. | **TOTAL TIME:** 11 hr., 40 min.

1   **Tbsp. kosher salt**
1   **Tbsp. ground black pepper**
½   **tsp. dried crushed red pepper**
3   **slabs baby back pork ribs (about 5½ lb.)**
2   **limes, halved**
Bottled barbecue sauce

1. Combine kosher salt and next 2 ingredients. Remove thin membrane from back of ribs by slicing into it with a knife and pulling it off. (This will make ribs more tender.)

2. Rub ribs with cut sides of limes, squeezing as you rub. Massage salt mixture into meat, covering all sides. Wrap tightly with plastic wrap. Place in a 13- x 9-inch baking dish; cover and chill 8 hours.

3. Light 1 side of grill, heating to 350° to 400° (medium-high) heat; leave other side unlit. Let ribs stand at room temperature 30 minutes. Remove plastic wrap. Place ribs over unlit side of grill, stacking 1 on top of the other. Grill, covered with grill lid, 40 minutes. Rotate ribs, moving bottom slab to top; grill 40 minutes. Rotate again; grill 40 minutes.

4. Lower grill temperature to 300° to 350° (medium) heat; place ribs side by side over unlit side of grill. Baste with barbecue sauce. Grill 30 minutes, covered with grill lid, basting occasionally with sauce. Remove from grill; let stand 10 minutes.

This recipe ensures fall-off-the-bone results every time.

Slow-Cooker Barbecue Pork

MAKES: 6 servings | **HANDS-ON TIME:** 10 min. | **TOTAL TIME:** 8 hr., 10 min.

1   **(3- to 4-lb.) boneless pork shoulder roast (Boston butt), trimmed**
1   **(18-oz.) bottle barbecue sauce**
1   **(12-oz.) can cola soft drink**

1. Place roast in a lightly greased 6-qt. slow cooker; pour barbecue sauce and cola over roast. Cover and cook on LOW 8 to 10 hours or until meat shreds easily with a fork.

2. Transfer pork to a cutting board; shred with two forks, removing any large pieces of fat. Skim fat from sauce, and stir in shredded pork.

Note: We tested with Cattleman's Original Barbecue Sauce.

Creamy Slaw

MAKES: 4 cups | **HANDS-ON TIME:** 5 min. | **TOTAL TIME:** 5 min.

1   **cup mayonnaise**
¼   **cup sugar**
2   **Tbsp. cider vinegar**
1   **tsp. refrigerated horseradish**
⅛   **tsp. salt**
⅛   **tsp. coarsely ground pepper**
1   **(16-oz.) package shredded coleslaw mix**

1. Stir together mayonnaise, sugar, and next 4 ingredients. Stir in coleslaw mix, stirring until blended. Cover and chill until ready to serve. Store in an airtight container in refrigerator up to 5 days.

For delicious sandwiches, serve Slow-Cooker Barbecue Pork on buns with additional sauce and top with Creamy Slaw.

For Cuban Sandwiches, layer Baked Pork Loin Roast slices with ham, Swiss, and mustard on bread, and cook in a panini press until cheese melts.

John Vaught was head football coach at Ole Miss from 1947-1970 (and also 1973). In 1959, Vaught led his squad to a national championship win.

Italian-Style Sandwiches

MAKES: 4 servings | **HANDS-ON TIME:** 15 min. | **TOTAL TIME:** 15 min., not including roast

1	(5.3-oz.) container spreadable goat cheese	1⅓	cups firmly packed arugula
2	Tbsp. refrigerated pesto with basil	½	cup jarred roasted red bell pepper strips
1	(12-oz.) package ciabatta rolls	¼	small red onion, thinly sliced
1	lb. thinly sliced Baked Pork Roast (about 24 slices)		

1. Stir together goat cheese and pesto. Spread goat cheese-and-pesto mixture on cut sides of rolls. Layer pork roast, arugula, and next 2 ingredients on bottom halves of rolls. Cover with top halves of rolls.

Note: We tested with Buitoni Pesto With Basil and Cobblestone Mill Ciabatta Rolls.

Barbecue Sandwiches

MAKES: 8 servings | **HANDS-ON TIME:** 10 min. | **TOTAL TIME:** 26 min., not including roast or slaw

1½	lb. thinly sliced Baked Pork Loin Roast (about 36 slices)	8	French hamburger buns Creamy Slaw (page 153)
1	(18-oz.) bottle spicy barbecue sauce		

1. Preheat oven to 375°. Stir together roast and barbecue sauce in a large skillet over medium-low heat. Cook, stirring occasionally, 8 to 10 minutes or until thoroughly heated.

2. Meanwhile, place buns on a baking sheet. Bake at 375° for 6 to 8 minutes or until golden brown. Cut buns in half lengthwise. Layer pork on bottom halves of buns. Top each with 1 heaping tablespoonful Creamy Slaw; cover with top halves of buns. Serve with remaining slaw.

 Extra Point: Save time and pick up shredded pork from your favorite BBQ restaurant. That's what we did for the cover recipe.

Baked Pork Loin Roast

MAKES: 8 to 10 servings | **HANDS-ON TIME:** 10 min. | **TOTAL TIME:** 2 hr.

1	(3- to 4-lb.) boneless pork loin	2	tsp. salt
1	Tbsp. olive oil	2	tsp. pepper

1. Preheat oven to 350°. Trim roast. Pat dry. Rub roast with olive oil. Sprinkle with salt and pepper; place in an aluminum foil-lined 13- x 9-inch pan.

2. Bake at 350° for 1½ to 2 hours or until a meat thermometer inserted into thickest portion registers 150°. Let stand 15 minutes before slicing.

Cuban
Sandwiches

Italian-Style
Sandwiches

Barbecue
Sandwiches

Spicy Buffalo Wings

MAKES: 4 servings | **HANDS-ON TIME:** 35 min. | **TOTAL TIME:** 1 hr., including sauces

2½	lb. chicken wing pieces (wings already cut)	1 cup all-purpose flour
2	tsp. salt	Vegetable oil
¾	tsp. ground black pepper	Spicy Buffalo Sauce
¼	tsp. ground red pepper	Cool Ranch Sauce
¼	tsp. onion powder	Celery sticks

1. Sprinkle wings with salt and next 3 ingredients. Dredge in flour, shaking off excess.

2. Pour oil to depth of 2 inches into a large deep skillet; heat to 350°. Fry wings, in batches, 3 to 4 minutes on each side or until done. Drain on a wire rack over paper towels. Toss wings in Spicy Buffalo Sauce; serve immediately with Cool Ranch Sauce and celery sticks.

Spicy Buffalo Sauce

MAKES: 1¼ cups | **HANDS-ON TIME:** 15 min. | **TOTAL TIME:** 15 min.

1	(8-oz.) can tomato sauce	½ tsp. salt
1	(5-oz.) bottle hot sauce	½ tsp. sugar
1	tsp. Worcestershire sauce	¼ tsp. pepper

1. Cook all ingredients in a saucepan over medium heat 8 to 10 minutes or until slightly thickened.

Note: We tested with Cholula Original Hot Sauce.

Cool Ranch Sauce

MAKES: 1¼ cups | **HANDS-ON TIME:** 10 min. | **TOTAL TIME:** 10 min.

½	cup mayonnaise	¼ tsp. lemon zest
½	cup sour cream	2 tsp. fresh lemon juice
¼	cup buttermilk	1 garlic clove, minced
1	Tbsp. chopped fresh chives	

1. Whisk together all ingredients and salt and pepper until smooth.

 Extra Point: This sauce makes a great dip for assorted crudités, or you can also thin it with additional buttermilk and drizzle over salad greens.

Cool down these kicked-up wings with Ranch sauce and celery sticks.

Missouri Tigers players take the field at Memorial Stadium in Columbia, Missouri.

You can't beat Southern fried chicken for a day of football fun. Feel free to fry a day ahead of time to enjoy picnic-style.

Mama's Fried Chicken

MAKES: 4 to 6 servings | **HANDS-ON TIME:** 40 min. | **TOTAL TIME:** 2 hr., 40 min.

1	(3- to 4-lb.) whole chicken, cut into pieces	2	cups buttermilk
1	tsp. salt		Self-rising flour
1	tsp. pepper		Vegetable oil

1. Sprinkle chicken with salt and pepper. Place chicken in a shallow dish or zip-top plastic bag, and add buttermilk. Cover or seal, and chill 2 hours.

2. Remove chicken from buttermilk, discarding buttermilk. Dredge chicken in flour.

3. Pour oil to depth of 1½ inches in a deep skillet or Dutch oven; heat to 360°. Add chicken, a few pieces at a time; cover and cook 6 minutes. Uncover chicken, and cook 9 minutes. Turn chicken; cover and cook 6 minutes. Uncover and cook 5 to 9 minutes, turning chicken the last 3 minutes for even browning, if necessary. Drain on paper towels.

Spicy Honey-Lime Grilled Drumsticks

MAKES: 4 servings | **HANDS-ON TIME:** 15 min. | **TOTAL TIME:** 1 hr., 25 min., including sauce

8	chicken drumsticks	Spicy Honey-Lime Barbecue Sauce
1	tsp. salt	Garnishes: fresh cilantro leaves,
½	tsp. pepper	lime wedges
	Vegetable cooking spray	

1. Sprinkle chicken with salt and pepper. Let stand, covered, 30 minutes.

2. Coat cold cooking grate of grill with cooking spray, and place on grill. Preheat grill to 350° to 400° (medium-high) heat. Grill chicken, covered with grill lid, 5 to 10 minutes on each side or until browned. Reduce grill temperature to 250° to 300° (low) heat; grill chicken, covered with grill lid, 20 to 30 minutes.

3. Meanwhile, prepare Spicy Honey-Lime Barbecue Sauce. Reserve 1 cup sauce.

4. Brush chicken with remaining barbecue sauce. Cover with grill lid, and grill 10 more minutes or until done. Serve chicken with reserved 1 cup barbecue sauce.

The citrus and spice in these drumsticks are sure to win over any crowd. You can make the sauce ahead of time for easier tailgate prep.

Spicy Honey-Lime Barbecue Sauce

MAKES: about 2 cups | **HANDS-ON TIME:** 20 min. | **TOTAL TIME:** 20 min.

¼	cup butter	¼	cup honey
1	medium onion, diced (about 1 cup)	2	Tbsp. fresh lime juice
1	(12-oz.) bottle chili sauce	¼	tsp. pepper

1. Melt butter in a small saucepan over medium heat; add onion, and sauté 4 to 5 minutes or until tender. Stir in chili sauce, next 3 ingredients, and ⅓ cup water; bring to a boil. Reduce heat to low, and simmer 5 minutes. Store in refrigerator up to 1 week.

Mama's Fried Chicken

COME HOME TO
Mizzou-rah™!

The air sizzles with excitement
as alumni and fans gather along the streets in Columbia, Missouri, on a sunny Saturday to await the annual homecoming parade. "Hurray! Hurrah! Mizzou®! Mizzou!" they chant, happy to be back among friends.

"Homecoming defines Mizzou," says one proud Tiger. "It sums up everything it means to be a Missouri student, athlete, or fan: personal achievement, academic excellence, competitive greatness, and social responsibility."

For more than a century, MU has invited alumni and friends to "come home" and celebrate. In 1911, athletic director Chester Brewer dreamed up the idea to generate support for the first home game against hated rival Kansas. More than 10,000 answered his call, and the modern homecoming-day celebration was born.

These days, homecoming is a two-week party, complete with intramural competitions, a Friday night pep rally, and the much anticipated parade. Missouri fans even bleed for their school—a three-day blood drive extracts nearly 5,000 pints from MU's sturdiest stock.

Tradition runs deep at Faurot Field—a.k.a. "The Zou"—and one could argue every game day is homecoming. Before the season starts, freshmen whitewash the "Big M" that marks the north end zone. Tailgates feature mouthwatering Kansas City- or St. Louis-style barbecue, and thousands greet the Fighting Tigers as they make their way to the stadium before a game.

Missouri enjoys as much team support as any team in the nation. As they say here: Once a Tiger, always a Tiger!

MU historical records mention using crimson and gold as its school colors. But any true Tiger fan knows the official colors are black and gold—the colors of a Bengal tiger.

Columbia, MO

MISSOURI

> "The people here really embrace the university. It's a perfect college town."

Founded in 1839, the University of Missouri® was the first public university west of the Mississippi River.

The ghostly remains of Academic Hall, the first University of Missouri building, stand in the center of Francis Quadrangle. These six columns no longer support a structure, but for every student on the campus in Columbia, Missouri, they become an enduring symbol of their alma mater and the principles upon which it was built.

"Mizzou is steeped in tradition," says alum Dustin Jeffries, "and it all begins right here. In a fall ceremony, incoming freshmen rush south through The Columns to symbolize coming in from society. In May, seniors retrace their steps north through The Columns, back into society. These are defining moments for students."

Education has always been one of the economic pillars of the city of Columbia. From the beginning, the founding fathers planned to have a state university here, so they set aside land in the town's original plans. The city even beat out competitors by raising three times as much seed money to start the school.

Today, Mizzou is one of the country's finest academic institutions, and the school's black and gold are inseparably woven into the fabric of the city. "They call this Tiger Town," Dustin says.

BBQ, Brews, and Music with a Side of Art

One of the things that makes Columbia so wonderful is **Shakespeare's Pizza**. A *Good Morning America* poll named Shake's the best college hangout in the nation. There's no table service. Customers place their orders and pick them up when called, but the fresh, whole wheat crust is tossed and topped where everyone can see. The Masterpiece, a hand-tossed pie with a full portion of every basic topping on the menu, ranks high on the list of favorites. "Shakespeare's is one thing that Columbians agree on," Dustin says. "This family-owned restaurant just opened its third location. Just thinking about their pizza makes my mouth water!"

Katy Trail

Like any college town, CoMo has its share of watering holes. When the Tigers win, fans tear down the goal posts and march them through the streets to **Harpo's**, where bartenders keep hacksaws to cut pieces for souvenirs. Opened in 1884, **Booche's Billiard Hall** still serves small yet delicious burgers delivered on wax paper. (Bring cash—they don't take credit cards.) **Flat Branch Pub & Brewing** is the place for burgers, brick-oven pizza, and locally brewed suds. Signature brews include Katy Trail Pale Ale and the Green Chili Beer spiced with Anaheim and serrano peppers.

The debate rages on about who has the best barbecue in town—**Buckingham Smokehouse Bar-B-Q** and **Bandana's Bar-B-Q** both have a following. After a game, **D. Rowe's**

hearty portions satisfy fans. **Broadway Diner** is a classic for comfort food and breakfast; locals and students favor The Stretch, a mix of hash browns, eggs, chili, cheese, green peppers, and onion. Another landmark, **Ernie's Café**, also serves a terrific breakfast.

For live music, head to **The Blue Note** or its little sister **Mojo's** for up-and-coming artists. Not only is **Addison's** a favorite for a nice dinner, it's a great place for night owls too. The evening happy hour begins at 10 p.m. nightly and features half-price appetizers. While there, check out the artwork by bartender David Spear.

Riding the Trails—by Bike or on Foot

Autumn is the perfect time to hike or bike Missouri's **Katy Trail,** the longest rail trail in the country. The 240-mile state park stretches from Machens to Clinton along the right-of-way of the former Missouri-Kansas-Texas Railroad. Columbia is accessible via the M.K.T. Trail, a 9-mile spur off the main path.

For more information: **Columbia Convention & Visitors Bureau, 800/652-0987** or **573/875-1231**.

Broadway Diner

Missouri Tigers® Menu

Spicy Buffalo Wings
with Spicy Buffalo Sauce
and Cool Ranch Sauce (page 157)

Cowboy Nachos
(recipe below)

Tiger Stripe Brownie Sundaes
(page 243)

Sack 'em with a plate of nachos loaded with braised brisket and Monterey Jack.

Cowboy Nachos

MAKES: 6 to 8 servings | **HANDS-ON TIME:** 30 min. | **TOTAL TIME:** 35 min., not including brisket and pico de gallo

2	(16-oz.) cans seasoned pinto beans, drained
2	tsp. hot sauce
1	tsp. minced garlic
½	tsp. freshly ground pepper
3½	cups shredded Braised Beef Brisket (page 150)
1	Tbsp. canola oil
½	cup taco sauce
¼	cup pan drippings from Braised Beef Brisket*
1	(9-oz.) package round tortilla chips
1	(8-oz.) block Monterey Jack cheese, shredded
	Pico de Gallo (page 93)
	Toppings: guacamole, sour cream, pickled jalapeño pepper slices

1. Preheat oven to 425°. Cook first 4 ingredients and ½ cup water in a medium saucepan over medium-low heat, stirring occasionally, 5 to 7 minutes or until thoroughly heated.

2. Cook brisket in hot oil in a skillet over medium heat, stirring often, 4 minutes or until thoroughly heated. Stir in taco sauce and pan drippings; cook 2 minutes.

3. Divide chips, bean mixture, brisket mixture, cheese, and 1 cup Pico de Gallo among 3 pie plates.

4. Bake at 425° for 5 minutes or until cheese is melted. Serve immediately with remaining Pico de Gallo and desired toppings.

*¼ cup beef broth may be substituted.

Note: Nachos can be baked as directed in 2 batches on an aluminum foil-lined baking sheet, topping each batch with 1 cup Pico de Gallo.

Low and slow brings out the mouthwatering barbecue flavor in this recipe. You can even make the chicken ahead, reheat, and serve over the Sweet Potato Cornbread.

Slow-Cooked BBQ Chicken Sandwiches

MAKES: 6 servings | **HANDS-ON TIME:** 20 min. | **TOTAL TIME:** 5 hr., 30 min., not including cornbread, peppers and onions, and slaw

2	tsp. salt	¼	cup firmly packed light brown sugar
1½	tsp. paprika		
½	tsp. garlic powder	2	Tbsp. apple cider vinegar
½	tsp. pepper	2	Tbsp. bourbon
1	(3- to 3½-lb.) cut-up whole chicken	1	lemon, sliced
½	cup cola soft drink		Sweet Potato Cornbread (page 167)
⅓	cup ketchup		Pickled Peppers & Onions
			Simple Slaw (page 167)

1. Stir together first 4 ingredients in a small bowl. Sprinkle over chicken. Place chicken in a single layer in a lightly greased 6-qt. slow cooker.

2. Whisk together cola soft drink and next 4 ingredients in a small bowl. Slowly pour mixture between chicken pieces (to avoid removing spices from chicken). Place lemon slices in a single layer on top of chicken.

3. Cover and cook on HIGH 5 hours (or on LOW 6½ to 7½ hours) or until done.

4. Remove chicken from slow cooker, and let cool slightly (about 10 to 15 minutes). Discard lemons. Skin, bone, and shred chicken. Skim fat from pan juices, and pour over chicken. Serve chicken over sliced Sweet Potato Cornbread. Top with Pickled Peppers & Onions and Simple Slaw.

Note: To make ahead, cool shredded chicken completely. Label and freeze in an airtight container up to 3 months.

Pickled Peppers and Onions

MAKES: 1 qt. | **HANDS-ON TIME:** 20 min. | **TOTAL TIME:** 1 hr., 35 min., plus 24 hr. for chilling

½	small red onion, cut into ¼-inch-thick slices	½	green bell pepper, cut into ¼-inch-wide strips
	Ice water	1	cup white vinegar
½	red bell pepper, cut into ¼-inch-wide strips	6	Tbsp. sugar
		2	Tbsp. kosher salt
½	yellow bell pepper, cut into ¼-inch-wide strips	½	tsp. dried crushed red pepper

1. Soak onion slices in ice water to cover in a small bowl 10 minutes; drain. Place onion slices and bell pepper strips in 1 (1-qt.) canning jar.

2. Bring vinegar, next 3 ingredients, and 1 cup water to a boil in a small nonaluminum saucepan over medium-high heat, stirring occasionally, until sugar is dissolved.

3. Pour hot vinegar mixture over vegetables in jar. Let stand, uncovered, 1 hour. Cover and chill 24 hours. Store in an airtight container in refrigerator up to 1 week.

Sweet Potato Cornbread

MAKES: 6 servings | **HANDS-ON TIME:** 15 min. | **TOTAL TIME:** 50 min.

2	cups self-rising white cornmeal mix	2	cups cooked mashed sweet potatoes (about 1½ lb. sweet potatoes)
3	Tbsp. sugar		
¼	tsp. pumpkin pie spice	1	(8-oz.) container sour cream
5	large eggs	½	cup butter, melted

1. Preheat oven to 425°. Stir together first 3 ingredients in a large bowl; make a well in center of mixture. Whisk together eggs and next 3 ingredients; add to cornmeal mixture, stirring just until moistened. Spoon batter into a lightly greased 9-inch square pan.

2. Bake at 425° for 35 minutes or until golden brown.

Simple Slaw

MAKES: 6 servings | **HANDS-ON TIME:** 15 min. | **TOTAL TIME:** 15 min.

¼	cup apple cider vinegar	¼	tsp. pepper
¼	cup canola oil	¼	tsp. celery seeds
2	Tbsp. mayonnaise	1	(16-oz.) package shredded coleslaw mix
1	Tbsp. honey		
½	tsp. salt		

1. Whisk together first 7 ingredients in a large bowl. Stir in coleslaw mix. Serve immediately, or chill up to 24 hours.

Mango-Chicken Wraps

MAKES: 10 servings | **HANDS-ON TIME:** 15 min. | **TOTAL TIME:** 1 hr., 25 min.

⅔	cup vegetable broth	½	tsp. chopped and seeded serrano chile pepper (optional)
¼	cup chopped cilantro		
1	green onion, chopped	1½	lb. chicken breast strips
1	garlic clove	¼	tsp. salt
1	Tbsp. fresh lime juice (1 lime)		Romaine lettuce leaves
1	Tbsp. white wine vinegar	10	(8-inch) soft taco-size flour tortillas
½	tsp. sea salt		
2	fresh mangoes, peeled, chopped, and divided		Wooden picks (optional)

1. Process first 7 ingredients, 1 chopped mango, and, if desired, chile pepper in a food processor until smooth, stopping to scrape down sides. Pour half of cilantro mixture into a shallow dish or zip-top plastic freezer bag; add chicken. Cover or seal, and chill 1 hour. Cover, chill, and reserve remaining half of cilantro mixture.

2. Preheat grill to 350° to 400° (medium-high) heat. Remove chicken from marinade, discarding marinade. Sprinkle chicken with ¼ tsp. salt.

3. Grill chicken, covered with grill lid, 4 minutes on each side or until done.

4. Shred chicken into bite-size pieces. Stir together chicken, remaining chopped mango, and reserved cilantro mixture.

5. Place lettuce leaves on each tortilla, and top each with chicken mixture. Roll up tortillas, and secure with wooden picks, if desired.

The flavor combination in these mouthwatering Mango-Chicken Wraps will have fans coming back for more. You can prepare these wraps ahead of time for fuss-free food.

Smoky Chicken Panini with
Basil Mayo

Smoky Chicken Panini with Basil Mayo

MAKES: 4 servings | **HANDS-ON TIME:** 40 min. | **TOTAL TIME:** 50 min.

4	skinned and boned chicken breasts (about 1 lb.)
½	tsp. salt
⅛	tsp. freshly ground pepper
½	cup mayonnaise
2	Tbsp. chopped fresh basil
½	tsp. lemon zest
8	sourdough bread slices
½	lb. smoked Gouda cheese, sliced
1	cup loosely packed baby spinach
¼	cup thinly sliced sun-dried tomatoes
3	Tbsp. butter, melted

1. Preheat grill to 350° to 400° (medium-high) heat. Sprinkle chicken with salt and pepper. Grill chicken, covered with grill lid, 7 to 10 minutes on each side or until done. Let stand 10 minutes, and cut into slices.

2. Stir together mayonnaise and next 2 ingredients. Spread mixture on 1 side of each bread slice. Top 4 bread slices with chicken, Gouda, and next 2 ingredients. Top with remaining bread slices, mayonnaise mixture sides down. Brush sandwiches with melted butter.

3. Cook sandwiches, in batches, in a preheated panini press 2 to 3 minutes or until golden brown.

Parmesan-Pecan Fried Chicken

MAKES: 6 servings | **HANDS-ON TIME:** 30 min. | **TOTAL TIME:** 1 hr., 30 min.

2	lb. chicken breast tenders, cut into 1-inch-wide strips
1	cup buttermilk
1	cup ground pecans
⅔	cup plain yellow cornmeal
⅔	cup grated Parmesan cheese
1	Tbsp. Cajun seasoning
1	Tbsp. paprika
2	large eggs, beaten
	Vegetable oil

1. Place chicken and buttermilk in a large zip-top plastic freezer bag. Seal and chill 1 hour. Remove chicken from buttermilk, discarding buttermilk.

2. Combine pecans and next 4 ingredients in a shallow bowl. Dip chicken in eggs; dredge in pecan mixture, shaking off excess. Arrange on a baking sheet. Pour oil to depth of 1½ inches into a cast-iron Dutch oven or 12-inch (2¼-inch-deep) cast-iron skillet; heat to 350°. Fry chicken, in batches, 2 to 3 minutes or until golden brown and done. Drain on a wire rack over paper towels.

Note: We tested with Zatarain's Creole Seasoning.

Kick off your Saturday with gooey smoked Gouda, sun-dried tomatoes, and grilled chicken for a fresh spin on your standard sandwich.

Southern pecans and Cajun seasoning give this fried chicken its Southern accent. Enjoyed warm or cold, this down-home staple is sure to stand out at your tailgate, whether it's home or away.

Not a fan of blue cheese? You can substitute soft Brie. Pick up multigrain sourdough bread in the bakery section, or try using flaky croissants.

Pancetta-Arugula-Turkey Sandwiches

MAKES: 6 servings | **HANDS-ON TIME:** 15 min. | **TOTAL TIME:** 15 min.

12	multigrain sourdough bakery bread slices
5	oz. soft ripened blue cheese
1½	lb. sliced roasted turkey
½	cup whole-berry cranberry sauce
12	cooked pancetta slices
2	cups loosely packed arugula
¼	cup coarse-grained Dijon mustard

1. Spread 1 side of 6 bread slices with blue cheese. Layer with turkey, cranberry sauce, pancetta, and arugula. Spread 1 side of remaining 6 bread slices with mustard, and place, mustard sides down, on arugula.
Note: We tested with Saga Classic Soft-Ripened Blue-Veined Cheese.

Bacon-Horseradish-Turkey Sandwiches: Substitute 6 split croissants for bakery bread, 6 Havarti cheese slices for blue cheese, 6 cooked bacon slices for pancetta, and peach preserves for cranberry sauce. Stir 1 Tbsp. refrigerated horseradish into peach preserves. Proceed as directed.

Parmesan Chicken Salad

MAKES: 4½ cups | **HANDS-ON TIME:** 35 min. | **TOTAL TIME:** 1 hr.

½	cup chopped pecans
4	skinned and boned chicken breasts
1	tsp. salt
½	tsp. pepper
2	Tbsp. vegetable oil
¾	cup freshly grated Parmesan cheese
½	cup chopped celery
⅓	cup chopped green onions
¾	cup mayonnaise
2	Tbsp. spicy brown mustard
1	garlic clove, pressed

Garnish: curly leaf lettuce

1. Heat pecans in a large nonstick skillet over medium-low heat, stirring often, 6 to 8 minutes or until toasted and fragrant.
2. Sprinkle chicken with salt and pepper. Cook chicken in hot oil in skillet over medium-high heat 7 to 8 minutes on each side or until done; cool 20 minutes. Chop chicken.
3. Stir together chopped chicken, cheese, next 2 ingredients, and pecans.
4. Stir together mayonnaise, mustard, and garlic. Add to chicken salad; stir well. Cover and chill, or serve immediately.

Great for making the night before the big game, this cheesy chicken salad carries easily and can be enjoyed on a sandwich or by itself.

Pancetta-Arugula-Turkey
Sandwiches

Layered Cornbread Salad,
page 200

(7)
SIDELINE FAVORITES

No tailgate spread is complete without the side dishes. From potato salad and baked beans to grilled corn and crunchy coleslaw—these sensational sides will become the most requested repeats for every tailgating Saturday.

Mississippi Hush Puppies

MAKES: 1½ dozen | **HANDS-ON TIME:** 30 min. | **TOTAL TIME:** 30 min.

1 **cup self-rising cornmeal mix**
½ **cup self-rising flour**
1 **Tbsp. sugar**
1 **large egg**
½ **cup diced onion**
½ **cup chopped green bell pepper**
½ **cup milk or beer**
1 **jalapeño pepper, chopped**
Vegetable oil

1. Combine first 3 ingredients in a large bowl, and make a well in center of mixture.
2. Combine egg and next 4 ingredients, stirring well; add to dry ingredients, stirring just until moistened.
3. Pour oil to depth of 3 inches into a Dutch oven or large saucepan; heat to 375°.
4. Drop batter by rounded tablespoonfuls into hot oil, and fry, in batches, 2 minutes on each side or until golden brown. Drain on paper towels; serve immediately.

Even if you're not from Mississippi, you'll agree that nothing beats the taste of these crispy hush puppies.

Buttermilk Cornbread

MAKES: 8 servings | **HANDS-ON TIME:** 15 min. | **TOTAL TIME:** 45 min.

1¼ **cups all-purpose flour**
1 **cup plus 3 Tbsp. plain white cornmeal**
¼ **cup sugar**
1 **Tbsp. baking powder**
1 **tsp. salt**
¼ **cup butter, melted**
2 **large eggs**
1 **cup buttermilk**

1. Preheat oven to 400°. Heat an 8-inch cast-iron skillet in oven 5 minutes.
2. Meanwhile, whisk together first 5 ingredients in a bowl; whisk in melted butter. Add eggs and buttermilk, whisking just until smooth. Pour batter into hot, lightly greased skillet.
3. Bake at 400° for 30 to 33 minutes or until golden brown and cornbread pulls away from sides of skillet.

 Extra Point: Spread split wedges with pimiento cheese, and run under the broiler until melted for a delicious no-fuss appetizer.

Serve this Southern staple with soups, stews, or salads. Plan to make this just before guests arrive so they can enjoy it hot.

Mississippi Hush Puppies

Sour Cream Cornbread

MAKES: 8 servings | **HANDS-ON TIME:** 10 min. | **TOTAL TIME:** 30 min.

1½   **cups self-rising white cornmeal mix**
½   **cup all-purpose flour**
1   **(14¾-oz.) can low-sodium cream-style corn**
1   **(8-oz.) container reduced-fat sour cream**
3   **large eggs, lightly beaten**
2   **Tbsp. chopped fresh cilantro**
½   **cup (2 oz.) 2% reduced-fat shredded Cheddar cheese (optional)**

1. Preheat oven to 450°. Heat a 10-inch cast-iron skillet in oven 5 minutes.
2. Stir together cornmeal mix and flour in a large bowl; add corn and next 3 ingredients, stirring just until blended. Pour batter into hot, lightly greased skillet. Top with cheese, if desired.
3. Bake at 450° for 22 to 24 minutes or until golden brown and cornbread pulls away from sides of skillet.

Stir in finely diced jalapeño peppers for an added kick of heat.

Garlic-Herb Bread

MAKES: 8 servings | **HANDS-ON TIME:** 10 min. | **TOTAL TIME:** 25 min.

3   **garlic cloves, minced**
1   **Tbsp. chopped fresh chives**
2   **Tbsp. extra virgin olive oil**
2   **Tbsp. butter, melted**
½   **tsp. dried crushed red pepper**
1   **(16-oz.) French bread loaf**

1. Preheat oven to 350°. Stir together first 5 ingredients in a small bowl.
2. Cut bread in half lengthwise. Brush cut sides with garlic mixture; place on a baking sheet.
3. Bake at 350° for 13 to 15 minutes or until golden brown. Cut each bread half into 8 slices.

This crusty, flavorful bread rounds out whatever is on the menu—hot soups or even the Lowcountry Boil (page 134).

Sour Cream Cornbread

IF IT AIN'T SWAYIN',
We Ain't Playin'

"Game! Cocks®! Game! Cocks!"
The two sides of Williams-Brice Stadium™ scream at one another, begging the home team to show itself.

When the dramatic opening notes of "Also Sprach Zarathustra" suddenly blare from the speakers, the crowd of 80,000 gets louder. When the shroud drops from an oversize cage and reveals a larger-than-life rooster beating his chest, the roar becomes deafening. And when the South Carolina Fighting Gamecocks finally claim the field, the whole stadium shakes. Literally. Fans say if you look closely, you'll see the Upper East Deck sway. School officials added shock absorbers to alleviate safety concerns, but the shaking prompted former coach Joe Morrison to proclaim, "If it ain't swayin', we ain't playin'!"

South Carolina fans are as feisty as they come, just as you'd expect from a team named Gamecocks. Regardless of size or ability, true gamecocks are aggressive, territorial, and ready to fight. That sums up the game-day atmosphere at Williams-Brice—a.k.a. "The Cockpit"—when fans meet to spur on their team.

Avid tailgaters, fans of the Garnet and Black claim spots around the stadium and throughout the surrounding state fairgrounds. The well-heeled "railgate" at the famous Cockaboose Railroad, a caravan of parked cabooses on a stretch of dormant track renovated in 1990, parked just yards from the stadium entrance.

Like every SEC school, South Carolina is hungry for pigskin prominence. But win or lose, the faithful never ever fail to support their team. And that's something to crow about.

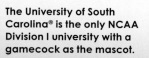

The University of South Carolina® is the only NCAA Division I university with a gamecock as the mascot.

GAMECOCKS

Columbia, SC

"The Horseshoe is the tie that binds the generations."

Over time, the Horseshoe's buildings—some from the early nineteenth century—have survived a fire, an earthquake, and the upheaval of the Civil War and Reconstruction.

Sunbeams slip through the canopy of oaks and fall in puddles of gold on the Horseshoe at the University of South Carolina in Columbia.

"When I was in school here," Bess Ware recalls, "the Horseshoe was our gathering place. We'd sit on the walls and wait for the boys to walk by. They'd stop and ask us to the dances. That's how we got our dates."

The Horseshoe remains the heart of the campus at South Carolina, as it has been since the school began in 1801. The founding fathers built the original buildings around a curved drive and surrounded it with lush lawns, red-brick paths, and sturdy walls. The buildings were used as a Confederate hospital and occupied by Union soldiers, and they've witnessed the shaping of some of the state's brightest minds.

"When I came to Carolina, we would study here or throw a Frisbee around," says Bess' daughter Barbara. "My mother was a freshman in 1935. I chose Carolina because I loved the stories she told about being a cheerleader and hanging out at the Horseshoe."

A Southern Smorgasbord

Today, two of the city's most vibrant neighborhoods—**Congaree Vista** and **Five Points**—hug the edges of the sprawling South Carolina campus. The Vista is a little more upscale and urbane, while students favor the more casual Five Points, but both offer enough restaurants, shops, and nightlife to keep visitors busy for days. "Just follow the crowd," says alum Frank Davis. "You can't go wrong in these neighborhoods."

When you see "Adluh" on a menu in Columbia, the item is made with flour or meal processed at the **Adluh Flour Mill** in The Vista. On weekdays, visitors can still stop by the mill office and buy their products. The historic Seaboard Train Station now houses **Blue Marlin**, a favorite for fresh-from-the-coast seafood. After a game,

Adluh Flour Mill

EdVenture

Gamecock fans gather at **Carolina Wings** or the rooftop bar at **Carolina Ale House**.

Both lunch and dinner menus change daily at **Motor Supply Company Bistro**, located in an old engine-supply warehouse. For small plates with big flavor, locals point to **Gervais & Vine**, a tapas and wine bar with an outdoor patio. **Nonnah's** is the go-to place for dessert, where selections range from Chocolate Temptation Cake to Deep Dish Apple Praline Pie.

Located in a flatiron-shaped building, **Yesterdays Restaurant and Tavern** is an icon in Five Points. The all-American menu features meatloaf, roast beef, and fried chicken, as well as down-home sides and delicious shrimp and grits. Now a regional chain, **Groucho's** started in Columbia with its dipper-style subs and array of delicious dipping sauces.

It's a goofy name, but locals adore **Mr. Friendly's New Southern Cafe**. The menu features fried green tomatoes, French Quarter pimiento cheese, and pecan crab cakes. And they serve homemade marshmallow-filled sandwich cookies on Mondays! **The Gourmet Shop** serves heavenly chicken salad, but it also doubles as a specialty foods store and kitchen shop that sells wine, cheese, olive oil, tableware, and utensils.

Family-Friendly Finds

Columbia is very family friendly too, and the **Riverbanks Zoo and Garden** tops the list. Visitors can see elephants, gorillas, and penguins, but there's also ample opportunity to interact with animals too. Kids can feed the giraffes or stroll through the kangaroo walk-about, plus there's a 70-acre botanical garden to explore. A child's imagination can also run free at **EdVenture**, the local children's museum.

For true nature lovers, the nearby **Congaree National Park** is a must. Visitors can canoe, kayak, or hike through the lowland swamp. The 2.4-mile Boardwalk Loop also gives less intrepid visitors an up-close view of this natural treasure, which includes the country's largest remaining bottomland hardwood forest.

For more information: **Columbia Metropolitan Convention and Visitors Bureau, 800/264-4884** or **803/545-0000**.

Gervais & Vine

South Carolina Gamecocks™ Menu

Warm Turnip Green Dip (page 92)

Grilled Blue Cheese-and-Bacon
Potato Salad (recipe below)

Southwestern Grilled Corn
(page 189)

Spicy Honey-Lime Grilled Drumsticks
(page 158)

Chocolate Marble Sheet Cake
(page 239)

Grilling the potatoes in an easy-to-fold aluminum foil packet adds a subtle note of smoky flavor— plus it makes cleanup a breeze.

Grilled Blue Cheese-and-Bacon Potato Salad

MAKES: 6 servings | **HANDS-ON TIME:** 20 min. | **TOTAL TIME:** 55 min.

3	lb. baby red potatoes, cut in half	¼	cup white balsamic vinegar
2	Tbsp. olive oil	2	tsp. sugar
1	tsp. salt	2	tsp. Dijon mustard
1	tsp. freshly ground pepper	1	cup thinly sliced red onion
1	cup mayonnaise	4	oz. crumbled blue cheese
¼	cup chopped fresh parsley	6	bacon slices, cooked and crumbled

1. Preheat grill to 350° to 400° (medium-high) heat. Place potatoes in a single layer in center of a large piece of heavy-duty aluminum foil. Drizzle with olive oil; sprinkle with salt and pepper. Bring up foil sides over potatoes; double fold top and side edges to seal, making 1 large packet.

2. Grill potatoes, in foil packet, covered with grill lid, 15 minutes on each side. Remove packet from grill. Carefully open packet, using tongs, and let potatoes cool 5 minutes.

3. Whisk together mayonnaise and next 4 ingredients in a large bowl; add potatoes, tossing gently to coat. Stir in onion, blue cheese, and bacon.

Cranberry-Almond
Coleslaw

Cranberry-Almond Coleslaw

MAKES: 8 servings | **HANDS-ON TIME:** 15 min. | **TOTAL TIME:** 15 min.

¼	cup apple cider vinegar	1	cup chopped smoked
2	Tbsp. Dijon mustard		almonds
2	Tbsp. honey	¾	cup sweetened dried
¾	tsp. salt		cranberries
¼	tsp. freshly ground pepper	4	green onions, sliced
¼	cup canola oil	2	celery ribs, sliced
2	(10-oz.) packages shredded coleslaw mix		

1. Whisk together first 5 ingredients. Gradually add oil in a slow, steady stream, whisking constantly until blended. Stir together coleslaw mix and next 4 ingredients in a large bowl; add vinegar mixture, tossing to coat.

Root Beer Baked Beans

MAKES: 4 servings | **HANDS-ON TIME:** 23 min. | **TOTAL TIME:** 1 hr., 18 min.

3	bacon slices	¼	cup hickory-smoked
1	small onion, diced		barbecue sauce
2	(16-oz.) cans pork and beans	½	tsp. dry mustard
½	cup root beer (do not use diet)	⅛	tsp. hot sauce

1. Preheat oven to 400°. Cook bacon in a large skillet over medium heat 8 to 10 minutes or until crisp; remove bacon, and drain on paper towels, reserving 2 Tbsp. drippings in skillet. Crumble bacon.

2. Sauté diced onion in hot bacon drippings over high heat 5 minutes or until tender. Stir together onion, crumbled bacon, beans, and remaining ingredients in a lightly greased 1-qt. baking dish.

3. Bake beans, uncovered, at 400° for 55 minutes or until sauce is thickened.

Root beer isn't only for drinking and ice-cream floats—it's also tasty in these sweet baked beans.

BLT Potato Salad

MAKES: 8 to 10 servings | **HANDS-ON TIME:** 20 min. | **TOTAL TIME:** 4 hr., 15 min.

3　large baking potatoes (about 3½ lb.), peeled and chopped
1　cup mayonnaise
1　Tbsp. chopped fresh parsley
3　Tbsp. sweet pickle relish
2　Tbsp. Dijon mustard
¾　tsp. salt
¾　tsp. freshly ground pepper
1　cup grape tomatoes, halved
3　green onions, sliced
2　hard-cooked eggs, peeled and chopped
4　bacon slices, cooked and crumbled
Lettuce leaves

1. Bring potatoes and salted water to cover to a boil in a Dutch oven. Boil 15 minutes or until tender. Drain and cool (about 30 minutes).

2. Stir together mayonnaise and next 5 ingredients in a large bowl; add cooked potatoes, tomatoes, green onions, and eggs, tossing gently until well blended. Cover and chill 3 hours. Stir in bacon just before serving. Serve on lettuce leaves.

Mexican-Style Grilled Corn

MAKES: 6 servings | **HANDS-ON TIME:** 15 min. | **TOTAL TIME:** 25 min.

6　ears fresh corn with husks
Kitchen string
2　Tbsp. reduced-fat mayonnaise
2　Tbsp. fat-free sour cream
3　Tbsp. finely grated Parmesan cheese
1　to 2 Tbsp. chili powder
2　limes, cut into wedges
Vegetable cooking spray
1½　tsp. salt
1　tsp. pepper

1. Light one side of grill, heating to 350° to 400° (medium-high) heat; leave other side unlit.

2. Pull back husks from corn; remove and discard silks. Tie husks together with kitchen string to form a handle.

3. Stir together mayonnaise and sour cream in a small bowl. Place Parmesan cheese, chili powder, and lime wedges in small serving bowls.

4. Coat each corn cob lightly with cooking spray. Sprinkle corn with salt and pepper. Position corn on cooking grate of grill so that tied husks lie over unlit side (to prevent burning husks).

5. Grill corn, covered with grill lid, 10 minutes or until golden brown, turning occasionally. Place corn on a platter. Spread with mayonnaise mixture, and sprinkle with cheese and chili powder. Squeeze lime wedges over corn.

Placing the corn husks over the unlit side of the grill allows you to omit the soaking step and saves time.

BLT Potato Salad

Sweet Potato Chips

Sweet Potato Chips

MAKES: 6 to 8 servings | **HANDS-ON TIME:** 40 min. | **TOTAL TIME:** 1 hr.

2   sweet potatoes, peeled (about 2 lb.)
Peanut oil
Kosher salt

1. Cut sweet potatoes into 1/16-inch-thick slices, using a mandoline. Pour peanut oil to depth of 3 inches into a Dutch oven; heat over medium-high heat to 300°. Fry potato slices, in small batches, stirring often, 4 to 4½ minutes or until crisp. Drain on a wire rack over paper towels. Immediately sprinkle with desired amount of kosher salt. Cool completely (about 20 minutes), and store in an airtight container at room temperature up to 2 days.

The secret to crisp sweet potato chips is to fry them in small batches in peanut oil at a low temperature.

Southwestern Grilled Corn

MAKES: varies | **HANDS-ON TIME:** 10 min. | **TOTAL TIME:** 35 min.

Desired number of ears of fresh corn with husks
Kitchen string
Melted butter
Salt
Chili powder
Smoked paprika
Grated Cotija or Parmesan cheese
Lime wedges

1. Preheat grill to 350° to 400° (medium-high) heat. Pull back husks from ears of fresh corn; remove and discard silks. Tie husks together with kitchen string to form a handle. Soak in cold salted water to cover 10 minutes; drain.
2. Grill corn, covered with grill lid, 15 minutes or until golden brown, turning occasionally. Remove from grill. Brush corn with melted butter; sprinkle with salt, chili powder, smoked paprika, and grated Cotija or Parmesan cheese. Serve with lime wedges.

Grilled Okra and Tomatoes

MAKES: 4 servings | **HANDS-ON TIME:** 20 min. | **TOTAL TIME:** 20 min.

1   lb. fresh okra, trimmed
1   pt. cherry tomatoes
2   Tbsp. olive oil
½   tsp. salt
½   tsp. pepper
2   Tbsp. chopped fresh basil

1. Preheat grill to 350° to 400° (medium-high) heat. Combine first 5 ingredients in a large bowl. Place mixture on cooking grate, and grill, covered with grill lid. Grill tomatoes 3 minutes or just until they begin to pop. Remove from grill. Turn okra, and grill, covered with grill lid, 2 to 3 more minutes or until tender.
2. Transfer okra and tomatoes to a serving dish, and sprinkle with basil. Serve immediately.

Double or triple the recipe for Grilled Okra and Tomatoes to serve a crowd.

Fried Green Tomatoes

Fried Green Tomatoes

MAKES: 6 servings | **HANDS-ON TIME:** 35 min. | **TOTAL TIME:** 35 min.

1	large egg, lightly beaten	½	cup all-purpose flour
½	cup buttermilk	3	medium-size, firm green
½	cup self-rising cornmeal		tomatoes (about 1¼ lb.),
	mix		cut into ⅓-inch-thick slices
½	tsp. salt		Vegetable oil
½	tsp. pepper		

1. Whisk together egg and buttermilk. Combine cornmeal mix, salt, pepper, and ¼ cup flour in a shallow dish. Dredge tomato slices in remaining ¼ cup flour; dip in egg mixture, and dredge in cornmeal mixture.

2. Pour oil to depth of ½ inch in a large cast-iron skillet; heat over medium-high heat to 375°. Drop tomatoes, in batches, into hot oil, and cook 2 minutes on each side or until golden. Drain on paper towels. Sprinkle hot tomatoes with salt to taste.

 Extra Point: For an impressive appetizer, stack tomatoes with goat cheese and cooked shrimp, and drizzle with balsamic vinaigrette. Delish!

Hot Bacon Potato Salad with Green Beans

MAKES: 8 servings | **HANDS-ON TIME:** 20 min. | **TOTAL TIME:** 45 min.

3	lb. fingerling potatoes, cut in half	1½	tsp. salt
1	(8-oz.) package haricots verts (tiny green beans)	1	tsp. pepper
		½	cup olive oil
½	cup white wine vinegar	¼	cup coarsely chopped fresh parsley
1	shallot, minced		
3	Tbsp. honey	2	Tbsp. chopped fresh dill
1	Tbsp. Dijon mustard	4	fully cooked bacon slices, chopped

1. Bring potatoes and water to cover to a boil in a large Dutch oven over medium-high heat, and cook 20 minutes or until tender. Drain.

2. Meanwhile, cook green beans in boiling water to cover in a medium saucepan 3 to 4 minutes or until crisp-tender. Plunge in ice water to stop the cooking process; drain.

3. Whisk together vinegar and next 5 ingredients in a medium bowl. Add oil in a slow, steady stream, whisking constantly until smooth.

4. Pour vinegar mixture over potatoes, and toss to coat. Just before serving, add green beans, parsley, and dill, and toss gently until blended. Sprinkle with bacon. Serve immediately, or cover and chill until ready to serve.

A Southern tailgate just isn't complete without a few key staples such as sweet tea, fried chicken, and, of course, fried green tomatoes. No doubt, these will please any true Southern football fan.

Grace your spread with this high-style potato salad. (Silver bowl optional!)

Broccoli, Grape, and Pasta Salad

MAKES: 6 to 8 servings | **HANDS-ON TIME:** 30 min. | **TOTAL TIME:** 3 hr., 35 min.

1	**cup chopped pecans**
½	**(16-oz.) package farfalle (bow-tie) pasta**
1	**lb. fresh broccoli**
1	**cup mayonnaise**
⅓	**cup sugar**
⅓	**cup diced red onion**
⅓	**cup red wine vinegar**
1	**tsp. salt**
2	**cups seedless red grapes, halved**
8	**cooked bacon slices, crumbled**

1. Preheat oven to 350°. Bake pecans in a single layer in a shallow pan 5 to 7 minutes or until lightly toasted and fragrant, stirring halfway through.

2. Prepare pasta according to package directions.

3. Meanwhile, cut broccoli florets from stems, and separate florets into small pieces using tip of a paring knife. Peel away tough outer layer of stems, and finely chop stems.

4. Whisk together mayonnaise and next 4 ingredients in a large bowl; add broccoli, hot cooked pasta, and grapes, and stir to coat. Cover and chill 3 hours. Season with salt to taste. Stir bacon and pecans into salad just before serving.

Creole Potato Salad

MAKES: 10 to 12 servings | **HANDS-ON TIME:** 35 min. | **TOTAL TIME:** 1 hr., 25 min.

5	**lb. baby red potatoes**
¼	**cup dry shrimp-and-crab boil seasoning**
12	**hard-cooked eggs, peeled and chopped**
1½	**cups finely chopped celery**
1	**cup finely chopped green onions**
1½	**Tbsp. Creole seasoning**
2	**cups mayonnaise**
⅓	**cup Creole mustard**

1. Bring potatoes, shrimp-and-crab boil, and 4 qt. water to a boil in a large stockpot over high heat. Boil 20 minutes or until tender; drain and cool 20 minutes.

2. Peel potatoes; cut into ¾-inch pieces. Toss together potatoes, eggs, and next 3 ingredients; stir in mayonnaise and mustard.

Note: We tested with Zatarain's Pro Boil and Tony Chachere's Creole Seasoning.

Fans cheer on the Vols in Neyland Stadium.

Broccoli, Grape, and Pasta
Salad

Apple-Walnut Salad

MAKES: 6 to 8 servings | **HANDS-ON TIME:** 20 min. | **TOTAL TIME:** 6 hr., 30 min.

1   cup chopped walnuts
⅔   cup mayonnaise
½   cup lemon curd
¼   tsp. ground cardamom
¼   tsp. ground nutmeg
⅛   tsp. ground cinnamon
1½   tsp. lemon zest
2   Gala apples, chopped
2   Granny Smith apples, chopped
2   Red Delicious apples, chopped
¾   cup thinly sliced celery
1   cup dried fruit mix

1. Preheat oven 350°. Bake walnuts in a single layer in a shallow pan 8 to 10 minutes or until toasted and fragrant, stirring once after 5 minutes.

2. Stir together mayonnaise, next 4 ingredients, and ½ tsp. lemon zest in a large bowl. Add apples, celery, fruit mix, and ¾ cup walnuts; toss well. Cover and chill 6 hours. Sprinkle with remaining ¼ cup walnuts and 1 tsp. lemon zest just before serving.

Note: We tested with Sun-Maid Fruit Bits.

Marinated Vegetable Salad

MAKES: 20 servings | **HANDS-ON TIME:** 20 min. | **TOTAL TIME:** 5 hr., 20 min.

1   (16-oz.) package fresh broccoli and cauliflower florets
1   (16-oz.) package cherry tomatoes
1   (15-oz.) can chickpeas, rinsed and drained
1   (6-oz.) can ripe black olives, drained and sliced
1   cup slivered snow peas
3   green onions, chopped
1   medium carrot, cut into thin strips
1   small red bell pepper, chopped
½   cup olive oil
⅓   cup red wine vinegar
2   garlic cloves, chopped
1½   tsp. chopped fresh or ½ tsp. dried basil
½   tsp. salt
½   tsp. sugar
¼   tsp. pepper
Garnish: fresh parsley sprig

1. Combine florets and next 7 ingredients in a large bowl.

2. Process oil and next 6 ingredients in a blender until smooth; add to vegetables, tossing to coat. Cover and chill 5 hours.

Combine an assortment of colorful vegetables and stir in chickpeas and olives for a hearty vegetable salad that's easy to make and easy to take.

Apple-Walnut Salad

IT'S FOOTBALL TIME IN ———
Tennessee!

"Oh, Rocky Top, you'll always be home sweet home to me-e," the masses sing with passion. "Good ole Rocky Top!"

Rocky Top, Tennessee. Population: 107,000. To a true Volunteer, there's no sweeter place on earth, especially come game day.

The fourth largest in the country, monstrous Neyland Stadium sits on the banks of the Tennessee River near downtown Knoxville. It's the Grand Canyon of the Southeastern Conference—climb to the summit and you can see all the way to the Smoky Mountains.

Long before a game starts, members of the Volunteer Navy pilot their boats upstream, dock across from the stadium, and form a giant floating tailgate party. Thousands more take the high ground to commune with family and friends.

By the time The Pride of the Southland Marching Band forms a long, narrow "T" that stretches from the 50-yard line to the north end zone checkerboard, anticipation has reached a fever pitch. When the team finally appears in the tunnel, the sea of orange parts. "As the 'T' opens to allow the team to run through, the crowd gets so loud you struggle to hear your own instrument," says one Pride alum.

This moment unites Volunteer fans the world over. "Game day at UT is the ultimate," says one. "So much goes on that you almost forget there's a game to play. But by the time the Vols run through the 'T' you remember—it's football time in Tennessee!"

Although "Rocky Top" is not the official fight song of the university, it's the most played and recognizable song associated with UT. It was written in 1967 by Felice and Boudleaux Bryant while they worked on tunes for another artist in Gatlinburg, Tennessee.

Knoxville, TN

VOLS

The Volunteer Navy gathers for a floating tailgate party

Fans who "tailgate" on the Tennessee River are referred to as the Volunteer Navy. They even have their own association, the VOL Navy Boaters Association.

A pedestrian mall on the University of Tennessee campus bears John Ward's name, but that's not where this alum's heart goes when he reminisces about UT.

It's not Neyland Stadium, either. "I think of Ayres Hall," says John, who for 31 years was the Voice of the Vols. "That's the University of Tennessee to me, believe it or not."

The Volunteers' signature orange and white colors reflect the daisies that are said to have once grown in abundance on The Hill, the heart of UT's old campus, where Ayres Hall still stands today. Tennessee's checkerboard end zones echo the architecture of Ayres' Gothic tower, and before every game, The Pride of the Southland Marching Band stops on its way to the stadium for a musical salute at the base of The Hill.

"There's nothing like Neyland Stadium and the Tennessee River on a Saturday afternoon in the fall," John continues. "It's a wonderful experience, and it is unique. But every student has walked up that hill to class. That's the true heart of the university."

UT anchors a city that was built by self-reliant, hardworking individuals who trekked over the mountains and put down roots on the side of a bluff in the Tennessee Valley. Though the city has expanded westward in recent years, downtown has also been revitalized and remains the heart of the city.

Game-Day Party Stops

Long the center of commerce, Knoxville's **Market Square** remains one of the most popular spots downtown. Home to excellent restaurants and shops, it also hosts special events throughout the year, including a local farmers' market on Saturdays through November. **Bliss** and **Bliss Home** showcase contemporary fashions and furnishings, while **Preservation**

Pub is a great place for beer and live music. Students and locals alike swear by **The Tomato Head** for gourmet sandwiches and pizza.

Fans of urban living flock to **Old City,** at the northeast corner of downtown, where old warehouses now host bars, restaurants, and high-end condos. Crowd-favorite **Barley's Taproom & Pizzeria** has some 50 craft-brewed beers on tap, as well as billiards, darts, and fresh sourdough pizza. **Crown & Goose** is a great local haunt too.

Closer to campus, **The Strip** is still a beacon to students and fans looking for a party. The lineup of bars and restaurants changes frequently, so just follow the crowd. Popular spots include **Copper Cellar, Gus's Good Time Deli, Old College Inn,** and **Cool Beans.**

Many fans simply confine their activities to Neyland Drive, which traces the route of the Tennessee River all the way from downtown to Kingston Pike. **Calhoun's on the River** is often packed on game days, thanks to its location just around the bend from the stadium, but an outdoor terrace and access to the

Great Smoky Mountains

Vol Navy make the wait downright enjoyable. House specialties include meaty baby back ribs and marinated-in-ale steaks.

Nature at Its Best

Though the city has more than 50 miles of greenways for walking, biking, and skating, fans use the **Neyland Greenway** to get to the stadium on game days. The world's largest basketball marks the location of the **Women's Basketball Hall of Fame,** where fans can test their skills and celebrate top female athletes, and the 10-acre **UT Trial Gardens** on the Ag Campus is a must-see for gardeners and shutterbugs.

Knoxville is second to none for natural beauty, thanks in large part to its proximity to the **Great Smoky Mountains.** The nation's most visited national park lies just an hour east of downtown on the Tennessee-North Carolina state line. Fall colors usually peak around the third week of October, but there's more to do here than sightsee. The area offers 850 miles of trails and unpaved roads for hiking plus ample room for horseback riding, biking, tubing, and fly-fishing.

"There are great universities all over the world," John says. "But there ain't no place like Knoxville."

For more information: **Knoxville Tourism & Sports Corporation, 800/727-8045.**

Neyland Greenway

Tennessee Volunteers® Menu

Rocky Top Popcorn (page 74)

Basil Tomato Soup (page 118)

Layered Cornbread Salad
(recipe below)

Smoky Chicken Panini with
Basil Mayo (page 169) or Italian-
Style Sandwiches (page 154)

Pineapple Upside-Down
Carrot Cake (page 241)

Layered Cornbread Salad

Make this crowd-pleaser up to one day ahead. Pair with grilled chicken for an easy and tasty weeknight meal.

MAKES: 6 servings | **HANDS-ON TIME:** 45 min. | **TOTAL TIME:** 3 hr., 55 min.

1	(6-oz.) package buttermilk cornbread mix	2	large yellow bell peppers, chopped
1	(12-oz.) bottle Ranch dressing	1	medium-size red onion, chopped
½	cup mayonnaise	1	cup diced celery (about 3 celery ribs)
¼	cup buttermilk		
1	tsp. coarsely ground pepper	2	cups (8 oz.) shredded Cheddar cheese
1	(10-oz.) package romaine lettuce, shredded	10	bacon slices, cooked and crumbled
2	large tomatoes, seeded and chopped	2	green onions, sliced

1. Prepare cornbread according to package directions; cool completely (about 25 minutes), and crumble. Stir together dressing, mayonnaise, buttermilk, and pepper until blended.

2. Layer shredded lettuce, crumbled cornbread, and next 6 ingredients in Mason jars or a 6-qt. bowl; spoon half of dressing mixture over top. Cover and chill 3 to 24 hours. Sprinkle with green onions just before serving. Serve with remaining half of dressing mixture on the side.

Note: We tested with Martha White Buttermilk Cornbread Mix.

Grilled Pear Salad

Grilled Pear Salad

MAKES: 6 to 8 servings | **HANDS-ON TIME:** 20 min. | **TOTAL TIME:** 20 min.

3   firm, ripe Bartlett pears, cut into ½-inch-thick wedges
¼   cup red wine vinegar
½   (10-oz.) jar seedless raspberry preserves
2   Tbsp. chopped fresh basil
1   garlic clove, pressed
½   tsp. salt
½   tsp. seasoned pepper
⅓   cup canola oil
1   (5-oz.) package gourmet mixed salad greens
½   small red onion, thinly sliced
2   cups fresh raspberries
¾   cup honey-roasted cashews
4   oz. crumbled goat cheese

1. Preheat grill to 350° to 400° (medium-high) heat. Grill pear wedges, covered with grill lid, 1 to 2 minutes on each side or until golden.

2. Whisk together red wine vinegar and next 5 ingredients in a small bowl; add canola oil in a slow, steady stream, whisking constantly until smooth.

3. Combine salad greens, next 4 ingredients, and pears in a large bowl. Drizzle with desired amount of vinaigrette, and toss to combine. Serve immediately with remaining vinaigrette.

> Grilling the pears heats the natural sugars, creating a nutty essence that balances with other ingredients.

Bread-and-Butter Pickles

MAKES: 10 (1-pt.) jars | **HANDS-ON TIME:** 55 min. | **TOTAL TIME:** 6 hr., 25 min.

6½   lb. small pickling cucumbers, cut into ¼-inch slices
      (about 33 cucumbers)
4   large sweet onions, thinly sliced
½   cup pickling salt
5   cups white vinegar (5% acidity)
4   cups sugar
2   Tbsp. mustard seeds
1½   tsp. ground turmeric
1   tsp. ground cloves
10   (1-pt.) canning jars

1. Combine cucumbers and onions in a very large Dutch oven; sprinkle with salt, and add water to cover (about 18 cups). Cover and let stand 3 hours. Drain well. Rinse with cold water.

2. Combine vinegar, sugar, mustard seeds, turmeric, and cloves in Dutch oven; cook over medium heat 5 minutes. Add cucumbers and onions; bring to a boil. Remove from heat.

3. Pack hot cucumber mixture into hot, sterilized jars, filling to ½ inch from top. Remove air bubbles; wipe jar rims. Cover at once with metal lids, and screw on bands. Process, in 2 batches, in boiling-water bath 12 minutes; cool completely (2 hours). Chill pickles before serving.

Bread-and-butter pickles make the perfect sandwich and burger toppers.

Pickled Okra

MAKES: 7 (1-pt.) jars | **HANDS-ON TIME:** 1 hr. | **TOTAL TIME:** 1 hr., plus 12 hr. for cooling

1	(9-piece) canning kit, including canner, jar lifter, and canning rack	7	garlic cloves
7	(1-pt.) canning jars	2	Tbsp. plus 1 tsp. dill seeds
2½	lb. small fresh okra	4	cups white vinegar (5% acidity)
7	small fresh green chile peppers	½	cup salt
		¼	cup sugar

1. Bring canner half-full with water to a boil; simmer. Meanwhile, place jars in a large stockpot with water to cover; bring to a boil, and simmer. Place bands and lids in a large saucepan with water to cover; bring to a boil, and simmer. Remove hot jars, 1 at a time, using jar lifter.

2. Pack okra into hot jars, filling to ½ inch from top. Place 1 pepper, 1 garlic clove, and 1 tsp. dill seeds in each jar. Bring vinegar, salt, sugar, and 4 cups water to a boil over medium-high heat. Pour over okra, filling to ½ inch from top.

3. Remove air bubbles. Wipe jar rims; cover at once with metal lids, and screw on bands (snug but not too tight). Place jars in canning rack, and place in simmering water in canner. Add additional boiling water as needed to cover by 1 to 2 inches.

4. Bring water to a rolling boil; boil 10 minutes. Remove from heat. Cool jars in canner 5 minutes. Transfer jars to a cutting board; cool 12 to 24 hours. Test seals of jars by pressing center of each lid. If lids do not pop, jars are properly sealed. Store in a cool, dry place at room temperature up to 1 year.

Nannie's Chowchow

MAKES: 12 (1-pt.) jars | **HANDS-ON TIME:** 40 min. | **TOTAL TIME:** 3 hr., 10 min., plus 8 hr. for chilling

2½	lb. green tomatoes, chopped (4 cups)	½	cup pickling salt
2	large yellow onions, chopped (4 cups)	1½	qt. white vinegar (5% acidity)
3	large green bell peppers, chopped (4 cups)	1½	cups sugar
2	red bell peppers, chopped (2¼ cups)	½	cup mustard seeds
1	(2½-lb.) cabbage, shredded (8 cups)	2	Tbsp. celery seeds
		1	Tbsp. whole allspice
		12	(1-pt.) canning jars

1. Combine first 5 ingredients in a large Dutch oven. Combine salt and 4 cups water; stir until salt dissolves. Pour over vegetables in Dutch oven. Chill 8 hours. Drain vegetables; discard liquid.

2. Combine vinegar and next 4 ingredients in Dutch oven; add vegetables. Bring to a boil over medium heat; reduce heat to medium-low, and simmer, covered, 10 minutes.

3. Pack hot mixture into hot, sterilized jars, filling to ½ inch from top. Remove air bubbles; wipe jar rims. Cover at once with metal lids, and screw on bands. Process in boiling-water bath 10 minutes; cool completely (about 2 hours).

Delicious pickled okra seasoned with garlic, chile peppers, and vinegar can be served alone or with a salad.

Enjoy this condiment year-round with meats and as a sandwich topper. For a fiery touch, add chopped jalapeños to the vegetables.

Mustard Butter

MAKES: about 1 cup | **HANDS-ON TIME:** 5 min. | **TOTAL TIME:** 5 min.

1   cup butter, softened
2   Tbsp. minced sweet onion
2   Tbsp. spicy brown mustard

1. Stir together all ingredients until blended.

 Extra Point: For a flavor boost, toss blanched green beans with Mustard Butter.

Watermelon, Mâche, and Pecan Salad

MAKES: 6 to 8 servings | **HANDS-ON TIME:** 20 min. | **TOTAL TIME:** 50 min., including vinaigrette

¾   cup chopped pecans
5   cups seeded and cubed watermelon
1   (6-oz.) package mâche

Pepper Jelly Vinaigrette
1   cup crumbled Gorgonzola cheese

1. Preheat oven to 350°. Bake pecans in a single layer on a baking sheet 5 to 7 minutes or until toasted and fragrant, stirring halfway through. Cool completely on a wire rack (about 15 minutes).
2. Combine watermelon and mâche in a large bowl; add vinaigrette, tossing gently to coat. Transfer watermelon mixture to a serving platter, and sprinkle with pecans and cheese.

Pepper Jelly Vinaigrette

MAKES: ¾ cup | **HANDS-ON TIME:** 10 min. | **TOTAL TIME:** 10 min.

¼   cup rice wine vinegar
¼   cup pepper jelly
1   Tbsp. fresh lime juice
1   Tbsp. grated onion
1   tsp. salt
¼   tsp. pepper
¼   cup vegetable oil

1. Whisk together first 6 ingredients. Gradually add oil in a slow, steady stream, whisking until blended.

 Extra Point: This is also terrific drizzled over a summery trio of sliced tomatoes, cucumbers, and onion.

Mâche, a tender heirloom variety of lamb's lettuce, has a slightly sweet, nutty flavor, but the salad is equally good prepared with baby lettuces.

THE HOG HEAVEN (ARKANSAS):
1½ inch strips of cooked bacon and
chopped fresh chives

THE CAVIAR TEASER (TEXAS A&M): Drained
and rinsed canned black-eyed peas, minced pickled
jalapeño peppers, and fresh cilantro leaves

THE BLUEGRASS SPECIAL
(KENTUCKY): Thinly sliced
country ham and a spot
of Dijon mustard

THE GATOR BAIT GOBBLER
(FLORIDA): Smoked salmon,
sour cream, and fresh dill

THE BLACK AND GOLD
PRIDE (MISSOURI): A generous
amount of freshly ground pepper

Team Deviled Eggs

Add your favorite team topping
just before serving.

THE RAGIN' CAJUN
(LSU): Peeled and cooked
shrimp, sliced celery, Cajun
seasoning, and a dash of hot sauce

THE SWEET-HEAT EAGLE EYE (AUBURN):
Sweet-hot pickle slices

THE GEORGIA PEACH (GEORGIA): Fresh peach slices, chopped Vidalia onion, and chopped toasted pecans

THE COWBELL (MISSISSIPPI STATE): Shaved red onion, sour cream, and capers

THE LOWCOUNTRY (SOUTH CAROLINA): Peeled cooked shrimp and Old Bay seasoning

Tailgate Deviled Eggs

MAKES: 12 servings | **HANDS-ON TIME:** 20 min. | **TOTAL TIME:** 20 min.

- **1 dozen hard-cooked eggs, peeled**
- **½ cup mayonnaise**
- **1 tsp. spicy brown mustard**

1. Slice eggs in half lengthwise, and carefully remove yolks. Reserve egg whites.

2. Mash yolks with mayonnaise and mustard until well blended. Add salt and pepper to taste. Spoon or pipe yolk mixture into reserved egg whites. Serve immediately, or cover and chill up to 1 day.

THE COMMODORE CHASER (VANDERBILT): Sliced black olives and chopped fresh parsley

THE BARBECUE BAMA SLAMMER (ALABAMA): Coarsely chopped smoked pulled pork drizzled with red and white 'cue sauce

THE SMOKY "T"-LITE (TENNESSEE): Smoky Pimiento Cheese (page 101)

THE HIGH SOCIETY (OLE MISS): Jumbo lump crabmeat, chopped fresh tarragon, freshly ground pepper, lemon zest, and a squeeze of fresh lemon

Hello Dolly Bars, page 224

(8)

THE SUGAR BOWL

Don't forget the sugar! Cakes, brownies, cookies, and pies make those clutch wins even sweeter. You'll be the star of the party when you serve these winning recipes.

Score big points and package an assortment of pralines in small white bakery boxes. Tie with string or ribbon in your team's colors.

Pecan Pralines

MAKES: 2 dozen | **HANDS-ON TIME:** 30 min. | **TOTAL TIME:** 1 hr., 15 min.

2   cups pecan halves and pieces
3   cups firmly packed light brown sugar
1   cup whipping cream
¼   cup butter
2   Tbsp. light corn syrup
1   tsp. vanilla extract
Wax paper

1. Preheat oven to 350°. Bake pecans in a single layer in a shallow pan 8 to 10 minutes or until toasted and fragrant, stirring halfway through. Cool completely (about 15 minutes).

2. Meanwhile, bring brown sugar and next 3 ingredients to a boil in a heavy Dutch oven over medium heat, stirring constantly. Boil, stirring occasionally, 6 to 8 minutes or until a candy thermometer registers 236° (soft ball stage). Remove sugar mixture from heat.

3. Let sugar mixture stand until candy thermometer registers 150° (20 to 25 minutes). Stir in vanilla and pecans using a wooden spoon; stir constantly 1 to 2 minutes or just until mixture begins to lose its gloss. Quickly drop by heaping tablespoonfuls onto wax paper; let stand until firm (10 to 15 minutes).

Chocolate-Pecan Pralines: Prepare recipe as directed through Step 2. Add 2 (1-oz.) unsweetened chocolate baking squares to sugar mixture. (Do not stir.) Proceed as directed in Step 3.

Café au Lait Pecan Pralines: Add 2 Tbsp. instant coffee granules with brown sugar in Step 2.

Bourbon-Pecan Pralines: Add ¼ cup bourbon with brown sugar in Step 2.

Bourbon Balls

MAKES: 4 dozen | **HANDS-ON TIME:** 5 min. | **TOTAL TIME:** 10 min.

1   (12-oz.) package vanilla wafers, finely crushed
1   cup chopped pecans or walnuts
¾   cup powdered sugar
2   Tbsp. unsweetened cocoa
½   cup bourbon
2½   Tbsp. light corn syrup
Powdered sugar

1. Stir together first 4 ingredients in a large bowl until well blended.

2. Stir together bourbon and corn syrup. Pour bourbon mixture over wafer mixture; stir until blended. Shape into 1-inch balls; roll in powdered sugar. Store in an airtight container up to 2 weeks.

Pecan Pralines

Crunchy Pecan Pie Bites

MAKES: about 6 dozen | **HANDS-ON TIME:** 15 min. | **TOTAL TIME:** 1 hr., 15 min.

- 3 **cups chopped pecans**
- ¾ **cup sugar**
- ¾ **cup dark corn syrup**
- 3 **large eggs, lightly beaten**
- 2 **Tbsp. melted butter**
- 1 **tsp. vanilla extract**
- ⅛ **tsp. salt**
- 5 **(2.1-oz.) packages frozen mini-phyllo pastry shells**

1. Preheat oven to 350°. Bake pecans in a single layer in a shallow pan 8 to 10 minutes or until toasted and fragrant, stirring halfway through.

2. Stir together sugar and corn syrup in a medium bowl. Stir in pecans, eggs, and next 3 ingredients.

3. Spoon about 1 heaping teaspoonful pecan mixture into each pastry shell, and place on 2 large baking sheets.

4. Bake at 350° for 20 to 22 minutes or until set. Transfer to wire racks, and cool completely (about 30 minutes). Store in an airtight container up to 3 days.

Mini Pecan Pies: Substitute 1½ (8-oz.) packages frozen tart shells for frozen mini-phyllo pastry shells. Prepare recipe as directed through Step 2. Spoon about ¼ cup pecan mixture into each tart shell. Place tart shells on a large baking sheet. Proceed with recipe as directed in Step 4, increasing bake time to 25 to 30 minutes or until set. Makes: 1 dozen. Hands-on Time: 15 min., Total Time: 20 min.

Peanut Butter Fudge

MAKES: about 1¾ lb. | **HANDS-ON TIME:** 20 min. | **TOTAL TIME:** 1 hr., 25 min.

- 1 **(5-oz.) can evaporated milk**
- 1⅔ **cups sugar**
- ½ **tsp. salt**
- 1¾ **cups miniature marshmallows**
- 1 **(10-oz.) package peanut butter morsels**
- 1 **tsp. vanilla extract**
- ½ **cup chopped peanuts**

1. Bring first 3 ingredients to a boil in a large saucepan over medium-high heat. Reduce heat to medium, and cook, stirring constantly, 5 minutes; remove from heat. Add marshmallows, peanut butter morsels, and vanilla; stir until smooth. Pour fudge into a greased 8-inch square pan. Gently press peanuts into top of warm fudge. Cool completely (about 1 hour). Cut into squares.

Crunchy Pecan Pie Bites

HOME OF THE
12th Man®

They whistle. They stomp. They scream. And don't bother telling them to sit down. As long as there are seconds on the clock, Aggie™ fans stand. When the game's on the line, they become the 12th Man.

Aggies love to tell how the tradition began. On January 2, 1922, A&M played top-ranked Centre College in a post-season matchup that would eventually become the Cotton Bowl. With reserves thinning, coach Dana X. Bible summoned a former player who was in the stands that day. Though E. King Gill didn't play a down in the Maroon and White's 22-14 victory, he stood suited and ready in case he was needed.

Today, Kyle Field is one of the loudest in college football. No fan base anywhere is more loyal, steadfast, and true than the one supporting Texas A&M University.

Other Aggieland traditions echo the university's rich military heritage. A&M's collie is named Reveille after the first mascot's penchant for barking when cadets were called to muster. The Fightin' Texas Aggie Band is the largest military marching band in the nation. And instead of cheerleaders, students elect male Yell Leaders who orchestrate Midnight Yells and keep the 12th Man energized during games.

Then there's the smooching. A&M men kiss their dates every time the Aggies score. "I still remember seeing my mom and dad kiss after every score," smiles one happy alum. "Now, kissing my wife is my favorite part of game day in College Station."

Texas A&M doesn't have cheerleaders. They have Yell Leaders. The Yell Leaders are comprised of five students elected by the student body each year.

College Station, TX

Legend has it that if a couple walks under the branches, they will eventually marry.

Over 100 years old, the Century Tree, a live oak, was one of the first trees planted on campus.

Texas A&M has more than its share of campus beauty spots.

"I love Academic Plaza," says 2006 graduate Molly Gage. "Silver Taps is played here every month for Aggies who have passed away, and the Century Tree is here too. It's a very peaceful place."

Her husband, Terry, has a real affinity for the Quadrangle on the south side of campus, where he lived as a member of the Corps of Cadets, the largest uniformed student body in the U.S. (outside the service academies). "The brick arches on the Quad symbolize the selfless sacrifice of Texas A&M's 12th Man, and that's really the spirit of Aggieland," he explains. "The Corps isn't A&M altogether, but it is the backbone of the university."

This is A&M

Still, Texas A&M is much more than a place to students and alumni. "You come to love Texas A&M because of what it is instead of what it looks like," Molly continues. "It's the traditions, the network, the loyalty. That's what we love most about A&M."

The first institution of higher education in the state, Texas A&M was planted along the tracks of the Houston and Texas Central Railway. In the early days, the train would stop to let young Aggies off at the so-called "college station" instead of the depot in nearby Bryan. Though it has matured into a city of more than 90,000, College Station retains its small-town atmosphere.

Definitive College Station

If there's a place that defines the town, it's the **Dixie Chicken** in the Northgate Entertainment District. The restaurant keeps a live rattlesnake on the premises and holds weekly dominoes tournaments, but the food keeps students and fans coming back for more. "There's no better place to get a burger and a cold beer," Terry says. "And don't forget the Tijuana Fries—hand-cut fries drenched in cheese, butter, and Ranch dressing. 'The Chicken' is definitely a staple in College Station."

Students also rave about **Antonio's Pizza by the Slice** and **Layne's Chicken Fingers**, and **Blue Baker** is "the place" for sandwiches and artisan bread. **La Bodega**, a Baja-style taco bar, is noted for its Mexican martinis (shaken margaritas) and fish tacos. Located in the original College Station City Hall building, **Café Eccell** offers brick-oven pizzas, but this is no college dive. The casual bistro features a fusion menu with entrées from gourmet street tacos to tortilla-encrusted snapper.

The Food and Drink Scene

College Station shares a border with the city of Bryan to the north. A twice-weekly **Farmers' Market** runs year-round, plus the historic downtown claims plenty of local shops and restaurants. Chef Christopher Lampo is the preferred caterer for former President Bush when he's in town, but visitors can sample his upscale fare at **Christopher's World Grille.**

For those with time to linger, Bryan's **Messina Hof Winery** is a must. The wines can be purchased at a number of local stores, but daily tours of the European-style winery and tastings make it worth the trek.

Presidential Pomp and Circumstance

Perhaps the most prestigious attraction in Aggieland can be found back on A&M's West Campus. Opened in 1997, the **George Bush Library and Museum** holds more than 44 million pages of documents and other artifacts from the 41st president's years of public service. "President and Mrs. Bush have an apartment above the library, and they stay there a lot," Molly notes. "They're very friendly people, and they're very immersed in the community, both in College Station and Houston."

For more information: **Bryan-College Station Convention and Visitors Bureau, 800/777-8292** or **979/260-9898.**

George Bush Library and Museum

Farmers' Market

Dixie Chicken

Texas A&M Aggies™ Menu

Spicy Queso Dip (page 92)

Layered Spicy Black Bean Dip
(page 91)

Guacamole (page 85)

Beef Fajitas with Pico de Gallo
(page 146)

Oven-Baked Churros
(recipe below)

Ready in 30 minutes, these baked churros are a treat that's ideal for coffee and cocoa dunking.

Oven-Baked Churros

MAKES: 3 dozen | **HANDS-ON TIME:** 15 min. | **TOTAL TIME:** 30 min.

1   (17.3-oz.) package frozen puff pastry sheets, thawed
Parchment paper
¼   cup sugar
1   tsp. ground cinnamon
¼   cup melted butter

1. Preheat oven to 450°. Unfold puff pastry sheets, and cut in half lengthwise. Cut each half crosswise into 1-inch-wide strips. Place strips on a lightly greased parchment paper-lined baking sheet. Bake 10 minutes or until golden brown.
2. Meanwhile, combine sugar and cinnamon. Remove pastry strips from oven, and dip in butter; roll in cinnamon-sugar mixture. Let stand on a wire rack 5 minutes or until dry.

All-Time Favorite Chocolate Chip Cookies

MAKES: about 5 dozen | **HANDS-ON TIME:** 30 min. | **TOTAL TIME:** 1 hr., 15 min.

¾ **cup butter, softened**
¾ **cup granulated sugar**
¾ **cup firmly packed dark brown sugar**
2 **large eggs**
1½ **tsp. vanilla extract**
2¼ **cups plus 2 Tbsp. all-purpose flour**

1 **tsp. baking soda**
¾ **tsp. salt**
1½ **(12-oz.) packages semisweet chocolate morsels**
Parchment paper

1. Preheat oven to 350°. Beat butter and sugars at medium speed with a heavy-duty electric stand mixer until creamy. Add eggs and vanilla, beating until blended.

2. Combine flour, baking soda, and salt in a small bowl; gradually add to butter mixture, beating just until blended. Beat in morsels just until combined. Drop by tablespoonfuls onto parchment paper-lined baking sheets.

3. Bake at 350° for 10 to 14 minutes or to desired degree of doneness. Transfer to wire racks, and cool completely (about 15 minutes).

Chocolate Chip-Pretzel Cookies: Prepare recipe as directed, beating in 2 cups coarsely crushed pretzel sticks with morsels.

White Chocolate-Covered Pretzel Cookies: Prepare recipe as directed, beating in 1 (7-oz.) package white chocolate-covered mini pretzel twists, coarsely crushed, with morsels.

Almond-Toffee Cookies: Substitute 6 (1.4-oz.) chopped chocolate-covered toffee candy bars and 1½ cups toasted slivered almonds for chocolate morsels. Proceed as directed.

Turtle Cookies: Substitute 1 (7-oz.) package milk chocolate-caramel-pecan clusters, coarsely chopped, and 1 (12-oz.) package dark chocolate morsels for semisweet chocolate morsels. Proceed as directed. **Note:** We tested with Nestlé Turtles.

If there was ever an official cookie of the SEC, this would be it. Best sports conference in the nation and best cookie ever—hands down.

Lee Nalley, a 1940s punt returner for the Vanderbilt Commodores, shows his skills at Vanderbilt Stadium in Nashville.

> Don't let the name fool you, these cookies are for everyone. Rich chocolate and ooey-gooey marshmallows have no team allegiance.

Mississippi Mud Cookies

MAKES: about 3 dozen | **HANDS-ON TIME:** 20 min. | **TOTAL TIME:** 40 min.

1	cup semisweet chocolate morsels	1	tsp. baking powder
½	cup butter, softened	½	tsp. salt
1	cup sugar	1	cup chopped pecans
2	large eggs	½	cup milk chocolate morsels
1	tsp. vanilla		Parchment paper
1½	cups all-purpose flour	1	cup plus 2 Tbsp. miniature marshmallows

1. Preheat oven to 350°. Microwave semisweet chocolate morsels in a small microwave-safe glass bowl at HIGH 1 minute or until smooth, stirring at 30-second intervals.

2. Beat butter and sugar at medium speed with an electric mixer until creamy; add eggs, 1 at a time, beating until blended after each addition. Beat in vanilla and melted chocolate.

3. Combine flour, baking powder, and salt; gradually add to chocolate mixture, beating until well blended. Stir in chopped pecans and ½ cup milk chocolate morsels.

4. Drop dough by heaping tablespoonfuls onto parchment paper-lined baking sheets. Press 3 marshmallows into each portion of dough.

5. Bake at 350° for 10 to 12 minutes or until set. Transfer to wire racks, and cool completely (about 20 minutes).

Peanut Butter-Toffee Turtle Cookies

MAKES: 3 dozen | **HANDS-ON TIME:** 20 min. | **TOTAL TIME:** 40 min.

⅔	cup creamy peanut butter	⅔	cup coarsely chopped peanuts
½	cup unsalted butter, softened	⅔	cup milk chocolate morsels
½	cup granulated sugar	10	oz. vanilla caramels
½	cup firmly packed light brown sugar	2	to 3 Tbsp. whipping cream
1	large egg	½	tsp. vanilla extract
2	cups all-purpose baking mix	⅔	cup milk chocolate morsels, melted
⅔	cup almond toffee bits		

1. Preheat oven to 350°. Beat first 4 ingredients at medium speed with an electric mixer until creamy. Add egg, beating until blended. Add baking mix, beating at low speed just until blended. Stir in toffee bits, chopped peanuts, and ⅔ cup chocolate morsels.

2. Drop dough by rounded tablespoonfuls onto ungreased baking sheets; flatten dough using your hands.

3. Bake at 350° for 10 to 12 minutes or until golden brown. Cool on baking sheets 1 minute; transfer to wire racks, and cool completely (about 20 minutes).

4. Microwave caramels and 2 Tbsp. cream in a glass bowl at HIGH 1 minute; stir. Continue to microwave at 30-second intervals, stirring until caramels melt and mixture is smooth, adding remaining 1 Tbsp. cream, if necessary. Stir in vanilla. Spoon caramel mixture onto cookies; drizzle with melted chocolate.

Note: We tested with Bisquick Original Pancake and Baking Mix.

These game-changing cookies are jam-packed with indulgent ingredients. The best part? You can bake a batch days in advance so that you're ready to go when it's time to tailgate.

Mississippi Mud Cookies

These easy seven-ingredient treats can be made a day ahead. Cut into bars just before serving.

Hello Dolly Bars

MAKES: about 3 dozen | **HANDS-ON TIME:** 15 min. | **TOTAL TIME:** 1 hr., 45 min.

2	**cups graham cracker crumbs**
⅓	**cup melted butter**
3	**Tbsp. sugar**
1	**cup chopped pecans**
1	**cup semisweet chocolate morsels**
⅔	**cup sweetened flaked coconut**
1	**(14-oz.) can sweetened condensed milk**

1. Preheat oven to 350°. Combine first 3 ingredients in a medium bowl. Press mixture onto bottom of a lightly greased 13- x 9-inch pan. Bake 8 minutes. Sprinkle pecans, chocolate morsels, and coconut over hot crust. Pour condensed milk over top. (Do not stir.)

2. Bake at 350° for 20 to 25 minutes or until lightly browned and edges are bubbly. Let cool on a wire rack 1 hour. Cut into bars.

Caramel-Pecan Bars

MAKES: about 2 dozen | **HANDS-ON TIME:** 30 min. | **TOTAL TIME:** 2 hr., 15 min.

3½	**cups coarsely chopped pecans**
2	**cups all-purpose flour**
⅔	**cup powdered sugar**
¾	**cup butter, cubed**
½	**cup firmly packed brown sugar**
⅔	**cup butter**
½	**cup honey**
3	**Tbsp. whipping cream**

1. Preheat oven to 350°. Line bottom and sides of a 13- x 9-inch pan with heavy-duty aluminum foil, allowing 2 to 3 inches to extend over sides. Lightly grease foil.

2. Bake pecans in a single layer in a shallow pan 8 to 10 minutes or until lightly toasted and fragrant, stirring halfway through.

3. Pulse flour, powdered sugar, and ¾ cup butter in a food processor 5 or 6 times or until mixture resembles coarse meal. Press mixture on bottom and ¾ inch up sides of prepared pan.

4. Bake at 350° for 20 minutes or until edges are lightly browned. Cool completely on a wire rack (about 15 minutes).

5. Bring brown sugar and next 3 ingredients to a boil in a 3-qt. saucepan over medium-high heat. Stir in toasted pecans, and spoon hot filling into prepared crust.

6. Bake at 350° for 25 to 30 minutes or until golden and bubbly. Cool completely on a wire rack (about 30 minutes). Lift baked bars from pan, using foil sides as handles. Transfer to a cutting board; cut into bars.

You'll be ready to take a bite out of the competition with these caramel-pecan treats.

Hello Dolly Bars

Tequila-Lime-Coconut
Macaroon Bars

Tequila-Lime-Coconut Macaroon Bars

MAKES: 3 dozen | **HANDS-ON TIME:** 20 min. | **TOTAL TIME:** 2 hr., 5 min.

- 2   **cups all-purpose flour, divided**
- 2   **cups sugar, divided**
- ½   **cup cold butter, cut into pieces**
- 4   **large eggs**
- 1½   **cups sweetened flaked coconut**
- 3   **Tbsp. tequila**
- 1   **tsp. lime zest**
- ⅓   **cup fresh lime juice**
- ½   **tsp. baking powder**
- ¼   **tsp. salt**

Garnishes: powdered sugar, lime rind curls

1. Preheat oven to 350°. Line bottom and sides of a 13- x 9-inch pan with heavy-duty aluminum foil, allowing 2 inches to extend over sides; lightly grease foil.

2. Stir together 1¾ cups flour and ½ cup sugar. Cut in butter with a pastry blender or fork until crumbly. Press mixture onto bottom of prepared pan.

3. Bake at 350° for 20 to 23 minutes or until lightly browned.

4. Meanwhile, whisk eggs in a medium bowl until smooth; whisk in coconut, next 3 ingredients, and remaining 1½ cups sugar. Stir together baking powder, salt, and remaining ¼ cup flour; whisk into egg mixture. Pour over hot crust.

5. Bake at 350° for 25 minutes or until filling is set. Cool on a wire rack 1 hour. Lift from pan, using foil sides as handles. Remove foil, and cut into bars.

These tangy-sweet bars are to-die-for. Think margarita meets piña colada in bar form.

Peach Melba Shortbread Bars

MAKES: 1½ to 2 dozen bars | **HANDS-ON TIME:** 20 min. | **TOTAL TIME:** 2 hr., 20 min.

- 2   **cups all-purpose flour**
- ½   **cup granulated sugar**
- ¼   **tsp. salt**
- 1   **cup cold butter**
- 1   **cup peach preserves**
- 6   **tsp. raspberry preserves**
- ½   **cup sliced almonds**

Garnish: powdered sugar

1. Preheat oven to 350°. Combine first 3 ingredients in a medium bowl. Cut in butter with a pastry blender until crumbly. Reserve 1 cup flour mixture.

2. Lightly grease an 11- x 7-inch or 9-inch square pan. Press remaining flour mixture onto bottom of prepared pan.

3. Bake at 350° for 25 to 30 minutes or until lightly browned.

4. Spread peach preserves over crust in pan. Dollop raspberry preserves by ½ teaspoonfuls over peach preserves. Sprinkle reserved 1 cup flour mixture over preserves. Sprinkle with almonds.

5. Bake at 350° for 35 to 40 minutes or until golden brown. Cool on a wire rack 1 hour. Cut into bars.

These standout shortbread bars pack all the flavor of the classic dessert in a handheld treat.

So-Good Brownies

MAKES: 16 servings | **HANDS-ON TIME:** 10 min. | **TOTAL TIME:** 1 hr., 50 min.

4	**(1-oz.) unsweetened chocolate baking squares**
¾	**cup butter**
1½	**cups granulated sugar**
½	**cup firmly packed brown sugar**
3	**large eggs**
1	**cup all-purpose flour**
1	**tsp. vanilla extract**
⅛	**tsp. salt**

1. Preheat oven to 350°. Line bottom and sides of an 8-inch pan with aluminum foil, allowing 2 to 3 inches to extend over sides; lightly grease foil.

2. Microwave chocolate squares and butter in a large microwave-safe bowl at HIGH 1½ to 2 minutes or until melted and smooth, stirring at 30-second intervals. Whisk in granulated and brown sugars. Add eggs, 1 at a time, whisking just until blended after each addition. Whisk in flour, vanilla, and salt.

3. Pour mixture into prepared pan.

4. Bake at 350° for 40 to 44 minutes or until a wooden pick inserted in center comes out with a few moist crumbs. Cool completely on a wire rack (about 1 hour). Lift brownies from pan, using foil sides as handles. Gently remove foil, and cut brownies into 16 squares.

Caramel-Macchiato Brownies: Stir 1 cup miniature marshmallows, ½ cup caramel bits*, and 1½ tsp. to 1 Tbsp. instant espresso powder into batter. Increase bake time to 44 to 46 minutes.
*12 caramels, quartered, may be substituted.
Note: Be sure to insert wooden pick into brownie, not marshmallow, when testing for doneness. (Marshmallows will rise to the top when baking.) We tested with Kraft Caramel Bits.

White Chocolate-Blueberry Brownies: Stir 1 (3.5-oz.) package dried blueberries and 1 (4-oz.) white chocolate baking bar, coarsely chopped, into batter. Increase bake time to 44 to 46 minutes.
Note: We tested with Sunsweet Dried Blueberries and Ghirardelli White Chocolate Baking Bar.

Toasted Coconut-Cashew Brownies: Spread 1 cup sweetened flaked coconut into a single layer on a baking sheet. Bake at 350° for 8 minutes or until lightly toasted, stirring every 2 minutes. Let cool 10 minutes. Stir toasted coconut; ½ cup cashews, chopped; and 2 Tbsp. finely chopped crystallized ginger into batter. Increase bake time to 44 to 46 minutes.

So-Good Brownies

TIME TO

Anchor Down

The Vanderbilt® quarterback fakes a hand off to his running back, hugs the ball close, and dives across the goal line. As the crowd erupts in celebration, a foghorn bellows from high atop the press box. Touchdown Commodores®!

To the faithful at Vanderbilt Stadium in Nashville, Tennessee, the sound of a ship's horn signaling a Commodore score is sweet music indeed and a grateful salute to a generous benefactor.

Vanderbilt bears the name of "Commodore" Cornelius Vanderbilt, the rail and shipping magnate from New York who provided the $1 million seed money to start the university in 1873 with the hope of helping to heal the wounds of the Civil War.

Today the university incorporates the nautical element of its history into its identity. The school's mascot, dubbed Mr. Commodore, sports a cutlass and mutton chops as he strides the sidelines. Two senior players lead the pregame Star Walk from the team locker room to the stadium carrying a gold anchor that symbolizes team unity. Fans christened their beloved naval horn The Admiral and fly a black flag emblazoned with a gold "V" over the stadium after victories.

Game days here begin with family-friendly activities and tailgating right next to the stadium, on the western edge of Vanderbilt's beautiful, park-like campus, just a couple of miles from downtown Nashville. As the sound of The Admiral calls fans of the Black and Gold to rally for kickoff and the Commodores take the field, foes best batten down the hatches as the 'Dores seek gridiron glory.

Vanderbilt cheerleaders
perform during a home
game at Vanderbilt Stadium.

Nashville, TN

"I can still hear that bell ring," says Whit Taylor, quarterback of the '82 Commodores®.
"Kirkland Hall is definitely the center of campus."

When Vanderbilt's first classes convened in 1875, the university was still self-contained in Kirkland Hall—then called Old Main.

There's poetry in the clock tower standing watch over Vanderbilt University, though few people even know it's there.

Kirkland Hall's tower hides a 1-ton bronze bell that marks the hours and calls students to class, just as it has since 1906. A message etched on the side of the bell reads: "Gift of the children to Vanderbilt University—1906—Ring in the Nobler Modes of Life."

Tennyson's words no doubt inspired those who commissioned this prodigious bell, as did the little souls who funded it. When Old Main, the original building on this spot, burned in 1905, the Nashville community came together to rebuild. Even the youngest citizens pitched in, donating their pennies to help purchase the bell. Their generous legacy echoes across campus every time the bell chimes.

Small School, Big City

Named for a former university chancellor, the Gothic building anchors the intimate 330-acre campus, an oasis of green in the midst of a city of more than half a million residents. "That's what's unique about Vanderbilt®," says Whit Taylor, quarterback of the '82 Commodores. "You are somewhat isolated because you're at a small school, but all around you is this big city."

Shaped like a fan, Vanderbilt's campus is tucked into a neighborhood less than 2 miles from rollicking downtown Nashville, with West End Avenue bordering one side and 21st Avenue South the other. Though chain restaurants and national retailers are beginning to dot the landscape here, hometown favorites still flourish.

Shakes, BBQ, Meat 'n' Three

Rotier's Restaurant claims a cult-like following for its milkshakes and mouthwatering cheeseburgers served on thick slabs of French bread. Those who follow the smell of hickory smoke find **Hog Heaven**. The menu is simple—barbecued pork, beef,

chicken, and turkey—but the Kickin' Chicken White Sauce is legendary. **Elliston Place Soda Shop**, an old-fashioned meat 'n' three, still serves soda fountain favorites including shakes, malts, and banana splits.

Go-To Food Spots

You can't talk about **Hillsboro Village,** the neighborhood across from Vanderbilt's medical campus, without mentioning the locally owned **Pancake Pantry**. Lines often stretch down the block, but this is still Nashville's "see and be seen" spot. **Fido** is the go-to coffee shop, and **McDougal's** specializes in fresh, hand-battered chicken fingers, wings, and hand-cut fries. The outdoor patio and innovative menu at **Jackson's Bar & Bistro** attract customers, while **Boscos** is the brewpub of choice. **Sunset Grill** is best known for its fine dining, but the restaurant offers a casual, budget-friendly, late-night menu too.

From Honky-Tonks to Broadway Lights

Nashville is called **Music City USA** for a reason. Musicians of every genre come here hoping to make it big,

Ryman Auditorium

which is really good news for visitors. From the **Schermerhorn Symphony Center** to the honky-tonks on Broadway, live music venues are plentiful. The weekly *Nashville Scene* publishes the lineup of who's playing.

The legendary **Ryman Auditorium** downtown is more than a museum. It's also still one of the best places to see a concert. Other hot spots include **The Wildhorse Saloon, Robert's Western World, Tootsie's Orchid Lounge,** and **The Stage.** The best new acts can be heard at the **Mercy Lounge** at the **Cannery Ballroom.**

A True Sports Town

Sports fans won't be able to leave town without checking the schedule at LP Field. Nashville is the only city that's home to both an SEC school and an NFL football team. If the **Tennessee Titans** aren't in town, shoot for a **Predators** game. The National Hockey League season starts in October.

For more information: **Nashville Convention & Visitors Bureau, 800/657-6910.**

Hog Heaven

Beer-Batter Fried Pickles
(page 77)

Sweet-Hot Baby Back Ribs (page 152)

Cranberry-Almond Coleslaw (page 185)

Mexican-Style Grilled Corn
(page 186)

Over-the-Moon Banana Pudding
(recipe below)

Soar over the competition with this mouthwatering marshmallow sandwich dessert. To transport, keep the pudding covered in a cooler until ready to serve.

Over-the-Moon Banana Pudding

MAKES: 12 to 15 servings | **HANDS-ON TIME:** 15 min. | **TOTAL TIME:** 2 hr., 45 min.

2   (4.6-oz.) packages cook-and-serve vanilla pudding mix
4   cups milk
1   (8-oz.) container sour cream
8   (2.75-oz.) chocolate-marshmallow sandwiches, cut into eighths
3   bananas, sliced
1   (8-oz.) container frozen whipped topping, thawed
Garnish: banana slices

1. Cook pudding mix and milk in a saucepan according to package directions. Remove pan from heat; let stand 10 minutes. Whisk in sour cream; let stand until pudding thickens (about 20 minutes).

2. Pour half of pudding into a 2-qt. baking dish. Layer about 40 chocolate-marshmallow sandwich wedges over pudding. Top with banana slices and remaining half of pudding. Top with whipped topping. Arrange remaining sandwich wedges around outer edge of dish. Cover and chill 2 hours or overnight.

Note: We tested with MoonPies for chocolate-marshmallow sandwiches and used Mini MoonPies around the edge of the baking dish for photo.

Hotty Toddy™, gosh almighty, this cake is good. The combination of chocolate, marshmallows, and pecans will have fans shouting for more.

Mississippi Mud Cake

MAKES: 15 servings | **HANDS-ON TIME:** 20 min. | **TOTAL TIME:** 2 hr., including frosting

1½	**cups coarsely chopped pecans**
2	**cups sugar**
1	**cup butter, melted**
½	**cup unsweetened cocoa**
4	**large eggs, lightly beaten**
1	**tsp. vanilla extract**
⅛	**tsp. salt**
1½	**cups all-purpose flour**
1	**(10.5-oz.) package miniature marshmallows**
	Chocolate Frosting

1. Preheat oven to 350°. Bake pecans in a single layer in a shallow pan 8 to 10 minutes or until toasted and fragrant, stirring halfway through.

2. Whisk together sugar and next 5 ingredients in a large bowl. Stir in flour and pecans. Pour batter into a greased and floured 15- x 10-inch jelly-roll pan.

3. Bake at 350° for 20 to 25 minutes or until a wooden pick inserted in center comes out clean. Remove from oven; top warm cake with marshmallows. Return to oven, and bake 5 minutes. Drizzle Chocolate Frosting over warm cake. Cool completely (about 1 hour).

Chocolate Frosting

MAKES: about 2 cups | **HANDS-ON TIME:** 15 min. | **TOTAL TIME:** 15 min.

½	**cup butter**
⅓	**cup unsweetened cocoa**
⅓	**cup milk**
1	**(16-oz.) package powdered sugar**
1	**tsp. vanilla extract**

1. Cook first 3 ingredients in a medium saucepan over medium heat until butter is melted. Cook, stirring constantly, 2 minutes or until slightly thickened; remove from heat. Beat in powdered sugar and vanilla at medium-high speed with an electric mixer until smooth.

The Fightin' Texas Aggie Band is nationally known for its marching formations and is the largest military marching band in the USA.

Vanilla Cupcakes with Cream Cheese Frosting

MAKES: 22 servings | **HANDS-ON TIME:** 20 min. | **TOTAL TIME:** 1 hr., 25 min., including frosting

1	cup butter, softened	1½	tsp. baking powder
2	cups sugar	¼	tsp. salt
3	large eggs	1	cup milk
1	tsp. vanilla extract	22	paper baking cups
2¾	cups all-purpose flour		Cream Cheese Frosting

1. Preheat oven to 350°. Beat butter at medium speed with an electric mixer until fluffy; gradually add sugar, beating well. Add eggs, 1 at a time, beating until blended after each addition. Add vanilla; beat until blended.

2. Combine flour, baking powder, and salt; add to butter mixture alternately with milk, beginning and ending with flour mixture. Beat at low speed just until blended after each addition. (Batter will be thick.)

3. Place 22 paper baking cups in 2 (12-cup) muffin pans; spoon ¼ cup batter into each cup.

4. Bake at 350° for 18 to 22 minutes or until a wooden pick inserted in center comes out clean. Remove from pans to wire racks, and cool completely (about 45 minutes). Pipe or spread Cream Cheese Frosting onto cupcakes.

Cream Cheese Frosting

MAKES: about 3 cups | **HANDS-ON TIME:** 5 min. | **TOTAL TIME:** 10 min.

½	cup butter, softened	1	(16-oz.) package powdered
1	(8-oz.) package cream cheese, softened		sugar
		1	tsp. vanilla extract

1. Beat butter and cream cheese at medium speed with an electric mixer until creamy. Gradually add powdered sugar, beating at low speed until blended; stir in vanilla.

Bayou Brownies

MAKES: about 3 dozen | **HANDS-ON TIME:** 15 min. | **TOTAL TIME:** 1 hr., 50 min.

1	(18.25-oz.) package yellow cake mix	1	(16-oz.) package powdered sugar
1	cup chopped pecans	1	(8-oz.) package cream cheese, softened
½	cup butter, melted		
3	large eggs, divided		

1. Preheat oven to 325°. Stir together first 3 ingredients and 1 egg until well blended; press onto bottom of a lightly greased 13- x 9-inch pan.

2. Beat powdered sugar, cream cheese, and remaining 2 eggs at medium speed with an electric mixer until smooth. Pour over cake mix.

3. Bake at 325° for 40 minutes or until set. Cool completely in pan on a wire rack (about 1 hour). Cut into squares.

Chocolate Marble Sheet Cake

MAKES: 12 servings | **HANDS-ON TIME:** 20 min. | **TOTAL TIME:** 1 hr., 50 min., including frosting

1	cup butter, softened	½	tsp. salt
1¾	cups sugar, divided	1	cup half-and-half
2	large eggs	¼	cup unsweetened cocoa
2	tsp. vanilla extract	3	Tbsp. hot water
2½	cups all-purpose flour		Mocha Frosting
1	Tbsp. baking powder		

1. Preheat oven to 325°. Beat butter and 1½ cups sugar at medium speed with a heavy-duty electric stand mixer 4 to 5 minutes or until creamy. Add eggs, 1 at a time, beating just until blended after each addition. Beat in vanilla.

2. Sift together flour, baking powder, and salt. Add to butter mixture alternately with half-and-half, beginning and ending with flour mixture. Beat at low speed just until blended after each addition, stopping to scrape bowl as needed.

3. Spoon 1¼ cups batter into a 2-qt. bowl, and stir in cocoa, 3 Tbsp. hot water, and remaining ¼ cup sugar until well blended.

4. Spread remaining vanilla batter into a greased and floured 15- x 10-inch jelly-roll pan. Spoon chocolate batter onto vanilla batter in pan; gently swirl with a knife or small spatula.

5. Bake at 325° for 23 to 28 minutes or until a wooden pick inserted in center comes out clean. Cool completely in pan on a wire rack (about 1 hour). Spread top of cake with Mocha Frosting.

To die for! Chocolate and vanilla mingle harmoniously in this mocha-topped marvel.

Mocha Frosting

MAKES: 2⅓ cups | **HANDS-ON TIME:** 10 min. | **TOTAL TIME:** 10 min.

3	cups powdered sugar	2	tsp. vanilla extract
⅔	cup unsweetened cocoa	½	cup butter, softened
3	Tbsp. hot brewed coffee	3	to 4 Tbsp. half-and-half

1. Whisk together sugar and cocoa in a medium bowl. Combine coffee and vanilla.

2. Beat butter at medium speed with a heavy-duty electric stand mixer until creamy; gradually add sugar mixture alternately with coffee mixture, beating at low speed until blended. Beat in half-and-half, 1 Tbsp. at a time, until smooth and mixture has reached desired consistency.

Mocha-Almond Frosting: Decrease vanilla extract to 1 tsp. Proceed with recipe as directed, adding ½ tsp. almond extract to coffee mixture in Step 1.

Nutter Butter®-Banana
Pudding Trifle

Nutter Butter®-Banana Pudding Trifle

MAKES: 8 to 10 servings | **HANDS-ON TIME:** 45 min. | **TOTAL TIME:** 3 hr., 15 min.

3	cups milk
3	large eggs
¾	cup sugar
⅓	cup all-purpose flour
2	Tbsp. butter
2	tsp. vanilla extract
5	medium-size ripe bananas

1 (1-lb.) package peanut butter sandwich cookies
2 cups sweetened whipped cream
Garnishes: peanut butter sandwich cookies, dried banana chips, fresh mint sprigs

1. Whisk together first 4 ingredients in a large saucepan over medium-low heat. Cook, whisking constantly, 15 to 20 minutes or until thickened. Remove from heat; stir in butter and vanilla until butter is melted.

2. Fill a large bowl with ice. Place saucepan in ice, and let stand, stirring occasionally, 30 minutes or until mixture is thoroughly chilled.

3. Meanwhile, cut bananas into ¼-inch slices. Break cookies into thirds.

4. Spoon half of pudding mixture into a 3-qt. bowl or pitcher. Top with bananas and cookies. Spoon remaining pudding mixture over bananas and cookies. Top with sweetened whipped cream. Cover and chill 2 to 24 hours.

Note: We tested with Nabisco Nutter Butter® Sandwich Cookies.

> This homemade layered pudding is divine, and uses on-hand staples. Peanut butter sandwich cookies take it over the top.

Pineapple Upside-Down Carrot Cake

MAKES: 8 servings | **HANDS-ON TIME:** 20 min. | **TOTAL TIME:** 1 hr., 15 min.

¼	cup butter
⅔	cup firmly packed brown sugar
1	(20-oz.) can pineapple slices in juice, drained
7	maraschino cherries (without stems)
1	cup granulated sugar
½	cup vegetable oil

2 large eggs
1 cup all-purpose flour
1 tsp. baking powder
1 tsp. ground cinnamon
¾ tsp. baking soda
½ tsp. salt
1½ cups grated carrots
½ cup finely chopped pecans

1. Preheat oven to 350°. Melt butter in a lightly greased 10-inch cast-iron skillet or a 9-inch round cake pan (with sides that are at least 2 inches high) over low heat. Remove from heat. Sprinkle with brown sugar. Arrange 7 pineapple slices in a single layer over brown sugar, reserving remaining pineapple slices for another use. Place 1 cherry in center of each pineapple slice.

2. Beat granulated sugar, oil, and eggs at medium speed with an electric mixer until blended. Combine flour and next 4 ingredients; gradually add to sugar mixture, beating at low speed just until blended. Stir in carrots and pecans. Spoon batter over pineapple slices.

3. Bake at 350° for 45 to 50 minutes or until a wooden pick inserted in center comes out clean. Cool in skillet on a wire rack 10 minutes. Carefully run a knife around edge of cake to loosen. Invert cake onto a serving plate, spooning any topping in skillet over cake.

Here's a pineapple upside-down cake with a twist: carrot cake.

Buttered Rum Pound Cake with Bananas Foster Sauce

MAKES: 10 to 12 servings | **HANDS-ON TIME:** 30 min. | **TOTAL TIME:** 7 hr., 10 min., including glaze and sauce

1	cup butter, softened
2½	cups sugar
6	large eggs, separated
3	cups all-purpose flour
¼	tsp. baking soda
1	(8-oz.) container sour cream

1	tsp. vanilla extract
1	tsp. lemon extract
½	cup sugar
	Buttered Rum Glaze
	Bananas Foster Sauce
	Vanilla ice cream

1. Preheat oven to 325°. Beat butter at medium speed with a heavy-duty electric stand mixer until creamy. Add 2½ cups sugar, beating 4 to 5 minutes or until fluffy. Add egg yolks, 1 at a time, beating just until yellow disappears.

2. Combine flour and baking soda; add to butter mixture alternately with sour cream, beginning and ending with flour mixture. Stir in extracts. Beat egg whites until foamy; gradually add ½ cup sugar, 1 Tbsp. at a time, beating until stiff peaks form and sugar dissolves. Fold into batter.

3. Pour batter into a greased and floured 10-inch tube pan.

4. Bake at 325° for 1½ hours or until a long wooden pick inserted in center comes out clean. Cool in pan 10 to 15 minutes; remove from pan, and place on a serving plate. While warm, prick cake surface at 1-inch intervals with a wooden pick; pour warm Buttered Rum Glaze over cake. Let stand 4 hours or overnight before serving. Serve with Bananas Foster Sauce and vanilla ice cream.

Buttered Rum Glaze

MAKES: 1¼ cups | **HANDS-ON TIME:** 15 min. | **TOTAL TIME:** 25 min.

½	cup chopped pecans	6	Tbsp. butter
¾	cup sugar	3	Tbsp. light rum

1. Preheat oven to 350°. Bake pecans in a single layer in a shallow pan 8 to 10 minutes or until toasted and fragrant, stirring halfway through.

2. Combine sugar, butter, rum, and 3 Tbsp. water in a small saucepan; bring to a boil. Boil, stirring constantly, 3 minutes. Remove from heat, and stir in pecans.

Bananas Foster Sauce

MAKES: 8 servings | **HANDS-ON TIME:** 10 min. | **TOTAL TIME:** 10 min.

½	cup firmly packed brown sugar	¼	tsp. ground cinnamon
⅓	cup banana liqueur	4	bananas, peeled and sliced
¼	cup butter, melted	⅓	cup light rum

1. Combine first 4 ingredients in a large skillet; cook over medium heat, stirring constantly, until bubbly. Add bananas, and cook 2 to 3 minutes or until thoroughly heated. Remove from heat.

2. Heat rum in a small saucepan over medium heat. (Do not boil.) Quicky pour rum over banana mixture, and carefully ignite the fumes just above mixture with a long match or long multipurpose lighter. Let flames die down; serve immediately.

This is the perfect finish for an at-home tailgating feast. The impressive Bananas Foster Sauce finish will rival even a last-second touchdown.

Utterly Deadly Pecan Pie

MAKES: 8 to 10 servings | **HANDS-ON TIME:** 10 min. | **TOTAL TIME:** 4 hr., 10 min.

½	(14.1-oz.) package refrigerated piecrusts	½	cup granulated sugar
1	Tbsp. powdered sugar	½	cup chopped pecans
4	large eggs	2	Tbsp. all-purpose flour
1½	cups firmly packed light brown sugar	2	Tbsp. milk
½	cup butter, melted and cooled to room temperature	1½	tsp. bourbon*
		1½	cups pecan halves

1. Preheat oven to 325°. Fit piecrust into a 10-inch cast-iron skillet; sprinkle piecrust with powdered sugar.
2. Whisk eggs in a large bowl until foamy; whisk in brown sugar and next 6 ingredients. Pour mixture into piecrust, and top with pecan halves.
3. Bake at 325° for 30 minutes; reduce oven temperature to 300°, and bake 30 more minutes. Turn oven off, and let pie stand in oven, with door closed, 3 hours.
*Vanilla extract may be substituted.

Serve this amazing pie straight out of the skillet. Top slices with vanilla ice cream.

Tiger Stripe Brownie Sundaes

MAKES: 8 servings | **HANDS-ON TIME:** 20 min. | **TOTAL TIME:** 2 hr., 15 min., including brownies and sauce

So-Good Brownies (page 228)   **Dark Chocolate Sauce**
Store-bought fudge-swirl vanilla ice cream

1. Top brownies with ice cream and Dark Chocolate Sauce. Serve immediately.

Dark Chocolate Sauce

MAKES: about 1 cup | **HANDS-ON TIME:** 5 min. | **TOTAL TIME:** 5 min.

1	(3-oz.) dark chocolate baking bar, chopped	¾	cup heavy cream

1. Microwave chocolate and cream in a small microwave-safe bowl at HIGH 1½ minutes or until melted and smooth, stirring every 30 seconds.

Extra Point: Use store-bought chocolate syrup in place of the Dark Chocolate Sauce, if traveling. Choose one that doesn't need to be warmed before serving. Place ice-cream cups in your cooler to keep them chilled during transit, and let guests assemble their own sundaes.

Lemonade Pie

MAKES: 8 servings | **HANDS-ON TIME:** 10 min. | **TOTAL TIME:** 4 hr., 10 min.

Cool off with a slice of one of the South's favorite refreshers.

2   **(5-oz.) cans evaporated milk**
2   **(3.4-oz.) packages lemon instant pudding mix**
2   **(8-oz.) packages cream cheese, softened**
2   **(3-oz.) packages cream cheese, softened**
1   **(12-oz.) can frozen lemonade concentrate, partially thawed**
1   **(9-oz.) ready-made graham cracker piecrust**
Garnishes: whipped cream, fresh mint sprigs, lemon slices, lemon rind strips

1. Whisk together evaporated milk and pudding mix in a bowl, whisking 2 minutes or until thickened.

2. Beat cream cheeses at medium speed with an electric mixer, using whisk attachment, until fluffy. Add lemonade concentrate, beating until blended; add pudding mixture, and beat until blended.

3. Pour into crust; freeze 4 hours or until firm.

Rebecca's Black Bottom Icebox Pie

MAKES: 8 to 10 servings | **HANDS-ON TIME:** 30 min. | **TOTAL TIME:** 9 hr.

Plan to serve this to guests at home, and get ready for plenty of compliments when you make this double-chocolate delight.

1   **(9-oz.) package chocolate wafers**
½   **cup butter, melted**
⅔   **cup sugar**
3   **Tbsp. cornstarch**
4   **egg yolks**
2   **cups milk**
2   **(4-oz.) bittersweet chocolate baking bars, chopped**
1   **Tbsp. dark rum**
1½   **tsp. vanilla extract**
2   **cups heavy cream**
¼   **cup sugar**
Garnish: bittersweet chocolate shavings

1. Pulse chocolate wafers in a food processor 8 to 10 times or until finely crushed. Stir together wafer crumbs and butter, and firmly press mixture on bottom, up sides, and onto lip of a lightly greased 9-inch pie plate. Freeze crust 30 minutes.

2. Whisk together ⅔ cup sugar and 3 Tbsp. cornstarch in a 3-qt. heavy saucepan.

3. Whisk together egg yolks and milk in a small bowl; whisk yolk mixture into sugar mixture in pan, and cook over medium heat, whisking constantly, 10 to 12 minutes or until mixture thickens. Cook 1 more minute. Remove from heat.

4. Microwave chocolate in a microwave-safe glass bowl at HIGH 1½ minutes or until melted, stirring at 30-second intervals. Whisk melted chocolate, rum, and vanilla into thickened filling. Spoon filling into prepared crust. Place plastic wrap directly onto filling (to prevent a film from forming), and chill 8 to 24 hours.

5. Beat heavy cream and ¼ cup sugar at medium-high speed with an electric mixer until soft peaks form. Top pie with whipped cream.

Note: We tested with Nabisco FAMOUS Chocolate Wafers and Ghirardelli 60% Cacao Bittersweet Chocolate Baking Bars.

Lemonade Pie

SEC Team Cupcakes

Go ahead. Choose sides, and create a stir with a batch of Vanilla Cupcakes with Cream Cheese Frosting (page 238). Once you declare your allegiance, spread state pride and school traditions liberally over these vanilla baked beauties.

MISSOURI: THE BLACK AND WHITE

Inspiration (Tiger stripes): Stir ½ cup melted dark chocolate morsels into half of frosting. Pipe cream cheese and chocolate frosting alternately onto each cupcake.

ALABAMA: THE ALABAMA LANE CAKE

Inspiration (The iconic Southern cake): Stir ¾ cup chopped toasted pecans, ¾ cup sweetened flaked coconut, ½ cup chopped golden raisins, and 1 tsp. orange zest into frosting. Garnish with maraschino cherries with stems.

TEXAS A&M: THE AMBROSIA

Inspiration (Ruby red grapefruit): Stir 3 tsp. red grapefruit zest, 1 Tbsp. red grapefruit juice, and 1½ cups sweetened flaked coconut into frosting. Garnish with orange and red grapefruit sections, sweetened flaked coconut, grapefruit rind curls, and fresh mint sprigs.

GEORGIA: THE PEANUT GALLERY

Inspiration (The state's bumper crop): Stir ¼ cup crunchy peanut butter into frosting. Garnish with peanut brittle.

OLE MISS: THE ITALIAN CREAM DREAM

Inspiration (Italian cream cake is as lush and indulgent as a tailgate on The Grove.): Stir 1 cup chopped toasted pecans and 1 cup sweetened flaked coconut into frosting. Garnish with sweetened flaked coconut and pecan halves.

FLORIDA: THE HUMMINGBIRD

Inspiration (Tropical fruits): Stir 1 cup chopped toasted pecans and ½ tsp. ground cinnamon into frosting. Garnish with fresh pineapple wedges, banana chips, and pecan halves.

LSU: THE MEAN MOCHA LATTE

MS STATE: THE LIGHTNING-FAST TURTLE

Inspiration (The state's pecan orchards): Garnish with toasted pecans and chocolate-covered caramel candies. Note: We tested with Rolo candies.

Inspiration (The state's famed French Quarter): Beat 1 Tbsp. instant espresso powder into frosting with butter. Garnish with chocolate-covered coffee beans and cocoa.

ARKANSAS: THE TRULY AMAZING MAPLE-BACON

Inspiration (The pork perfection of the mascot himself): Stir ½ tsp. maple extract into frosting. Garnish with cooked bacon pieces.

SOUTH CAROLINA: THE MILE-HIGH COCONUT

VANDERBILT: THE TENNESSEE JAM SESSION

Inspiration (Tennessee jam cake and the Music City): Melt 15 caramels with 1 Tbsp. milk; stir into frosting. Spread blackberry jam onto cupcakes, pipe with frosting. Garnish with fresh blackberries and fresh mint sprigs.

Inspiration (Lowcountry coconut layer cakes): Stir 1½ cups sweetened flaked coconut into frosting. Garnish generously with toasted coconut.

AUBURN: THE LEMONADE STAND

Inspiration (Toomer's Corner): Stir 2 tsp. lemon zest, 1 Tbsp. fresh lemon juice, and desired amount of yellow food coloring paste into frosting. Garnish with mini straws, lemon slices, and fresh mint sprigs.

TENNESSEE: THE ROCKY (ROAD) TOP

KENTUCKY: THE MINT CHOCOLATE CHIP

Inspiration (Mint juleps): Stir 1 tsp. peppermint extract and 1 (4-oz.) finely chopped bittersweet chocolate baking bar into frosting. Garnish with shaved thin crème de menthe chocolate mints and fresh mint sprigs.

Inspiration (The Great Smoky Mountains along the eastern Tennessee border): Stir 1 cup melted dark chocolate morsels into frosting. Garnish with miniature marshmallows, semisweet morsels, and toasted pecans.

Extra Point: You can find paper baking cups in a wide array of fun colors and designs. Customize for your specific team, if desired.

Metric Equivalents

The information in the following chart is provided to help cooks outside the United States successfully use the recipes in this book. All equivalents are approximate.

EQUIVALENTS FOR DIFFERENT TYPES OF INGREDIENTS

Standard Cup	Fine Powder (ex. flour)	Grain (ex. rice)	Granular (ex. sugar)	Liquid Solids (ex. butter)	Liquid (ex. milk)
1	140 g	150 g	190 g	200 g	240 ml
$3/4$	105 g	113 g	143 g	150 g	180 ml
$2/3$	93 g	100 g	125 g	133 g	160 ml
$1/2$	70 g	75 g	95 g	100 g	120 ml
$1/3$	47 g	50 g	63 g	67 g	80 ml
$1/4$	35 g	38 g	48 g	50 g	60 ml
$1/8$	18 g	19 g	24 g	25 g	30 ml

LIQUID INGREDIENTS BY VOLUME

$1/4$ tsp =				1 ml
$1/2$ tsp =				2 ml
1 tsp =				5 ml
3 tsp = 1 Tbsp =		$1/2$ fl oz =		15 ml
2 Tbsp = $1/8$ cup =	1 fl oz =			30 ml
4 Tbsp = $1/4$ cup =	2 fl oz =			60 ml
$5^{1/3}$ Tbsp = $1/3$ cup =	3 fl oz =			80 ml
8 Tbsp = $1/2$ cup =	4 fl oz =			120 ml
$10^{2/3}$ Tbsp = $2/3$ cup =	5 fl oz =			160 ml
12 Tbsp = $3/4$ cup =	6 fl oz =			180 ml
16 Tbsp = 1 cup =	8 fl oz =			240 ml
1 pt = 2 cups =	16 fl oz =			480 ml
1 qt = 4 cups =	32 fl oz =			960 ml
	33 fl oz =	1000 ml =	1 l	

DRY INGREDIENTS BY WEIGHT

(To convert ounces to grams, multiply the number of ounces by 30.)

1 oz = $1/16$ lb = 30 g
4 oz = $1/4$ lb = 120 g
8 oz = $1/2$ lb = 240 g
12 oz = $3/4$ lb = 360 g
16 oz = 1 lb = 480 g

LENGTH

(To convert inches to centimeters, multiply the number of inches by 2.5.)

1 in =			2.5 cm
6 in = $1/2$ ft =			15 cm
12 in = 1 ft =			30 cm
36 in = 3 ft = 1 yd =			90 cm
40 in =			100 cm = 1 m

COOKING/OVEN TEMPERATURES

	Fahrenheit	Celsius	Gas Mark
Freeze Water	32° F	0° C	
Room Temperature	68° F	20° C	
Boil Water	212° F	100° C	
Bake	325° F	160° C	3
	350° F	180° C	4
	375° F	190° C	5
	400° F	200° C	6
	425° F	220° C	7
	450° F	230° C	8
Broil			Grill

recipe index

menus index

Oxmoor House
VP, Publishing Director: Jim Childs
Editorial Director: Leah McLaughlin
Creative Director: Felicity Keane
Senior Brand Manager: Daniel Fagan
Senior Editor: Rebecca Brennan
Managing Editor: Rebecca Benton

***Southern Living® The Official SEC
    Tailgating Cookbook***
Senior Editor: Heather Averett
Project Editor: Sarah H. Doss
Senior Designer: Melissa Clark
Assistant Designer: Allison Sperando Potter
Junior Designer: Maribeth Jones

Director, Test Kitchen:
    Elizabeth Tyler Austin
Assistant Directors, Test Kitchen:
    Julie Christopher, Julie Gunter
Recipe Developers and Testers:
    Wendy Ball, R.D.; Victoria E. Cox;
    Stefanie Maloney; Callie Nash;
    Leah Van Deren
Recipe Editor: Alyson Moreland Haynes
Food Stylists: Margaret Monroe Dickey,
    Catherine Crowell Steele
Photography Director: Jim Bathie
Senior Photo Stylist: Kay E. Clarke
Photo Stylist: Katherine Eckert Coyne
Assistant Photo Stylist:
    Mary Louise Menendez
Production Manager: Theresa Beste-Farley

Contributors
Designer and Compositor: Teresa Cole
Writer: Cassandra M. Vanhooser
Photo Editor: Paula Gillen
Recipe Developers and Testers:
    Tamara Goldis, Erica Hopper,
    Kathleen Royal Phillips
Copy Editors: Donna Baldone, Ashley Leath
Proofreaders: Emily C. Beaumont,
    Dolores Hydock, Mary Ann Laurens
Indexer: Mary Ann Laurens
Interns: Erin Bishop, Mackenzie Cogle,
    Laura Hoxworth, Alicia Lavender,
    Anna Pollock, Emily Robinson,
    Ashley White
Food Stylist: Marian Cooper Cairns
Photographer: Jennifer Davick
Photo Stylist: Lydia Degaris Pursell

***Southern Living*®**
Editor: M. Lindsay Bierman
Creative Director: Robert Perino
Managing Editor: Candace Higginbotham
Art Director: Chris Hoke
Associate Art Director:
    Erynn Hedrick Hassinger

Executive Editors:
    Rachel Hardage Barrett, Jessica S. Thuston
Food Director: Shannon Sliter Satterwhite
Test Kitchen Director:
    Rebecca Kracke Gordon
Senior Writer: Donna Florio
Senior Food Editor: Mary Allen Perry
Recipe Editor: JoAnn Weatherly
Assistant Recipe Editor: Ashley Arthur
Test Kitchen Specialist/Food Styling:
    Vanessa McNeil Rocchio
Test Kitchen Professionals:
    Norman King, Pam Lolley,
    Angela Sellers
Directors of Photography: Julie Claire,
    Mark Sandlin
Style Director: Heather Chadduck
Senior Photographers: Ralph Lee
    Anderson, Gary Clark, Art Meripol
Photographers: Robbie Caponetto,
    Laurey W. Glenn
Photo Coordinator:
    Megan McSwain Yeatts
Photo Research Coordinator:
    Ginny P. Allen
Senior Photo Stylist: Buffy Hargett
Studio Assistant:
    Caroline Murphy Cunningham
Editorial Assistant: Pat York
Office Manager: Nellah Bailey McGough

Time Home Entertainment Inc.
Publisher: Richard Fraiman
VP, Strategy & Business Development:
    Steven Sandonato
Executive Director, Marketing Services:
    Carol Pittard
**Executive Director, Retail & Special
    Sales:** Tom Mifsud
**Director, Bookazine Development &
    Marketing:** Laura Adam
Executive Publishing Director: Joy Butts
Finance Director: Glenn Buonocore
Associate General Counsel: Helen Wan

To order additional publications, call 1-800-765-6400 or 1-800-491-0551.

For more books to enrich your life, visit **oxmoorhouse.com**

To search, savor, and share thousands of recipes, visit **myrecipes.com**

Cover: Barbecue Sandwiches (page 154)

Photo Credits

Page 1: Jeff Etheridge **Page 2:** (Row 1 left to right) University of Alabama/Collegiate Images/Getty Images; Wesley Hitt; Joe Robbins; (Row 2 left to right) Keff Jones; Streeter Lecka/Getty Images; ZUMA Wire Service/Alamy; Matthew Emmons/US PRESSWIRE; (Row 3 left to right) Robert Jordan/Ole Miss Communications; Butch Dill/Getty Images; Wesley Hitt/Getty Images; University of South Carolina Photo Services; (Row 4 left to right) Streeter Lecka/Getty Images; Texas A&M Division of Marketing & Communications; David Berman/Sports Illustrated/Getty Images **Page 3:** Courtesy of the Southeastern Conference **Page 6:** (top) Andrew Davis Tucker/University of Georgia; (bottom) Bob Rosato/Sports Illustrated/Getty Images **Page 9:** (top) Ray Carson; (bottom) Megan Smith **Page 10:** Carol M. Highsmith; William Stanley Hoole Special Collection **Page 14:** George Silk/Time Life Pictures/Getty Images **Page 18:** (top left) Greg Nelson/Sports Illustrated/Getty Images; (top right) David E. Klutho/Sports Illustrated/Getty Images; (center) Texas A&M Division of Marketing & Communications; (bottom left) Scott Cunningham/Getty Images; (bottom right) John Russell/Getty Images **Page 19:** (top right) Gary Bogdon/Sports Illustrated/Getty Images; (bottom left) Sean Allsopp; (bottom right) Derick E.

Hingle/ US PRESSWIRE **Page 25:** Carol M. Highsmith **Page 27:** Chip Litherland **Page 29:** (top) Carol M. Highsmith/ Library of Congress; (bottom left) Ronald C. Modra/ Getty Images; (bottom right) Courtesy Innisfree Pub **Page 33:** (bottom) William Stanley Hoole Special Collection/The University of Alabama Libraries **Page 36:** Wesley Hitt **Page 41:** Wesley Hitt **Page 42:** Wesley Hitt **Page 43:** (left) Courtesy James at the Mill **Page 48:** Heinz Kluetmeier/ Sports Illustrated/Getty Images **Page 50:** (top left) Mike Zarrilli/Getty Images **Page 53:** Carol M. Highsmith **Page 54:** Auburn University **Page 55:** (left) Caleb Colquitt; (top right) Michael Clemmer (bottom right) Todd J. Van Emst/Auburn Athletics **Page 59:** Keith Stephenson **Page 65:** Ray Carson/University of Florida **Page 66:** Lucian Badea/ARS Photographics **Page 67:** (top left) Ray Carson/University of Florida; top right: Emily Jourdan; bottom: Will McC/Wikimedia Commons **Page 79:** Terry Manier **Page 80:** Paul Efland, University of Georgia **Page 81:** (top left) Courtesy Elizabeth Vance; (bottom left) Courtesy Elliott Anderson/Caren West PR; (right) Amy Wallas Fox **Page 93:** (bottom) Walter Sanders/Time & Life Pictures/Getty Images **Page 95:** University of Kentucky Public Relations & Marketing **Page 96:** Glen Allison/Getty Images **Page 97:** (top) Mark Cornelison/Lexington Herald-Leader/Getty Images; (bottom) Courtesy Three Chimneys Farm **Page 111:** Crystal LoGiudice/US PRESSWIRE **Page 112:** Eddy Perez/LSU University Relations **Page 113:** (top) Courtesy The Chimes; (bottom) James Lemass/Getty Images **Page 116:** LSU Library/Special Collections **Page 123:** Mississippi State University Libraries **Page 125:** Kerry Smith/AP Photo **Page 126:** Megan Bean/Mississippi State University **Page 127:** (top right) Gordon Fikes;

(bottom left) Roger Smith **Page 130:** Butch Dill/Getty Images **Page 136:** Wesley Hitt/ Getty Images **Page 141:** Wesley Hitt/Getty Images **Page 142:** Wesley Hitt **Page 143:** (left) Brian T. Murphy; (top right) Holly Moore/HollyEats.com **Page 148:** Archives & Special Collections/University of Mississippi **Page 152:** (bottom) Marvin E. Newman/Sports Illustrated/Getty Images **Page 154:** Courtesy Ole Mississippi Sports **Page 157:** Jamie Squire/Getty Images **Page 161:** Wesley Hitt/Getty Images **Page 162:** Carol M. Highsmith **Page 163:** (bottom left) Wampa-One/Flckr; (bottom right) Mike Tigas **Page 179:** Wesley Hitt/Getty Images **Page 180:** University Technology Services/ USC **Page 181:** (top right) Earl C. Leatherberry; (bottom left) Courtesy EdVenture Museum; (bottom right) Courtesy Gervais & Vine **Page 192:** Gary Bogdon/Sports Illustrated/Getty Images **Page 197:** Streeter Lecka/Getty Images **Page 198:** Courtesy Volunteer Princess Cruises **Page 199:** (bottom left) Courtesy Steven Bridges/OutDoorKnoxville.com **Page 215:** Wesley Hitt **Page 216:** Texas A&M Division of Marketing and Communications **Page 217:** (top left) Anne Rippy/Getty Images; (bottom) Wikimedia Commons **Page 221:** Vanderbilt/Collegiate Images/Getty Images **Page 231:** Grant Halverson/Getty Images **Page 232:** Vanderbilt/Collegiate Images/ Getty Images **Page 233:** (bottom left) Courtesy Hog Heaven **Page 236:** Texas A&M Division of Marketing and Communications **Pages 254-255:** Mike Powell/Sports Illustrated/Getty Images **Endsheets:** Aaron M. Sprecher/AP Photo

The Southeastern Conference and its Corporate Sponsors Celebrate the Conference's Six Consecutive Football National Championships.